Sept. 14, 19

To: Marcia Volpert
With warmest good
wishes.

Neil C. Sandberg

And to my esteemed
friend and colleague,
Richard Volpert,
my profound appreciation
Neil

Jewish Life in Los Angeles

A Window to Tomorrow

Neil C. Sandberg

UNIVERSITY PRESS OF AMERICA

LANHAM • NEW YORK • LONDON

University Press of America,® Inc.

4720 Boston Way
Lanham, MD 20706

3 Henrietta Street
London WC2E 8LU England

Printed in the United States of America

Library of Congress Cataloging in Publication Data

Sandberg, Neil C.
Jewish life in Los Angelos.

Bibliography: p.
Includes index.
1. Jews—California—Los Angeles—Identity.
2. Jews—California—Los Angeles—Cultural assimilation.
3. Los Angeles (Calif.)—Ethnic relations. I. Title.
F869.L89J57 1986 305.8'924'079494 86-11025
ISBN 0-8191-5439-3 (alk. paper)

All University Press of America books are produced on acid-free paper which exceeds the minimum standards set by the National Historical Publications and Records Commission.

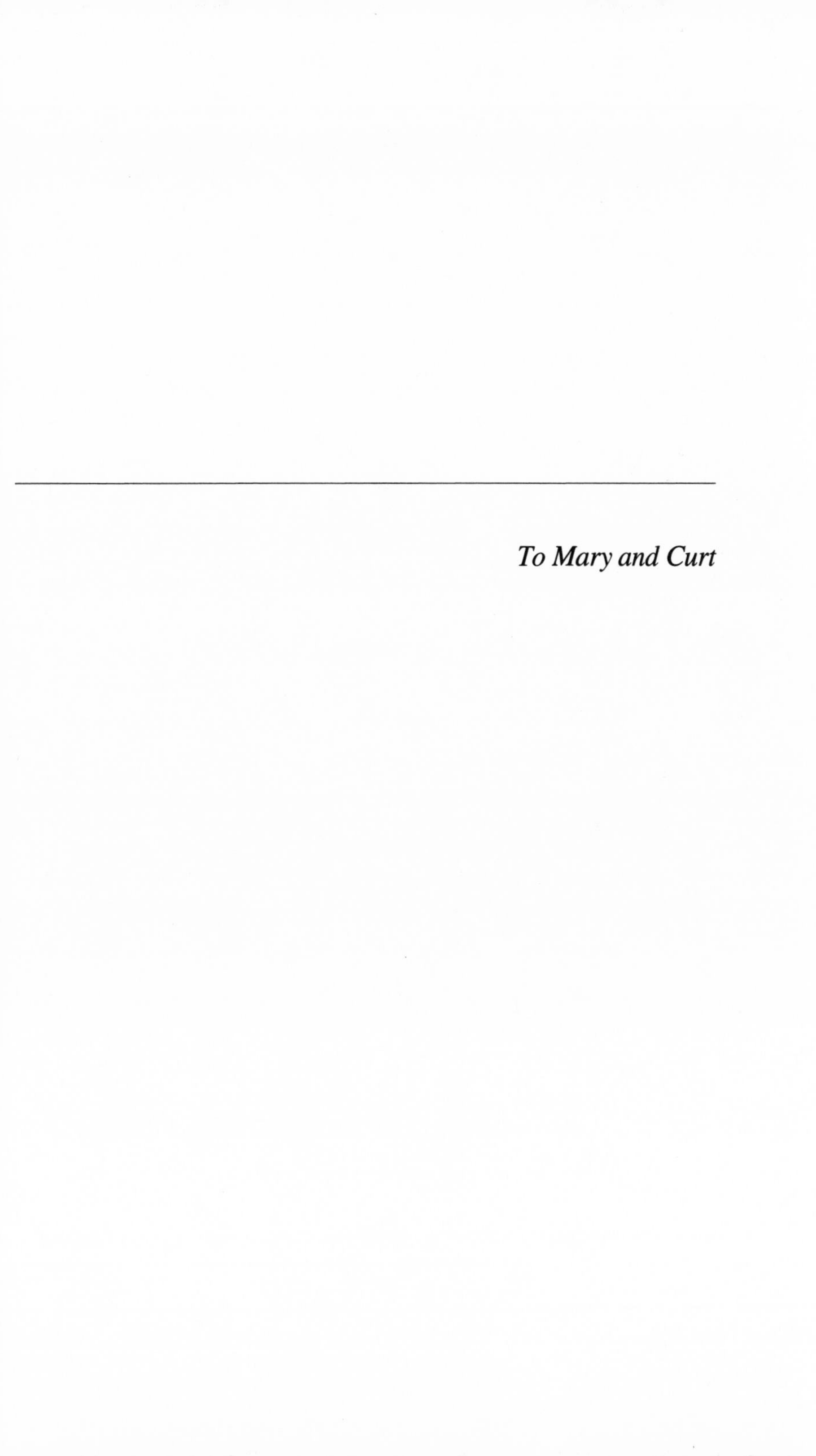

To Mary and Curt

Judaism or converted (see Table 9). The rate of intermarriage is much higher among unaffiliated Jews of all generations, rising to an extraordinary 66.7% among the unaffiliated of the fourth generation. While there is also an increase of intermarriage among affiliated Jews, the rate of growth is much lower and tends to level off between the third and fourth generations.

TABLE 9

AFFILIATED WITH A CONGREGATION, BY RELIGION OF SPOUSE

	Religion of Spouse	
Affiliated	[illegible]	Other
Yes	[illegible]	[illegible]
No	[illegible]	[illegible]
	[illegible]	[illegible]

[illegible]

The respondents were asked if any of their children had married non-Jews and 25.9% responded affirmatively. Intermarriage of children is highest among parents who have had the least Jewish education and, when examined by socioeconomic status, those at the very lowest and very highest ends of the scale show the lowest rates of intermarriage for their children. The data indicate that the highest rate of intermarriage is among the children of working and middle-class Jews, and the lowest is among those with the highest socioeconomic status (see Table 10). This suggests that for those in the highest SES group, their permissiveness toward interdating (see Table 8) is not yet reflected in the behavior of their children.

In regard to the responses of parents if their children were to marry non-Jews, there is relatively little opposition or resistance. Men, young people under thirty, those who are the least educated

Acknowledgements

A number of friends and colleagues in the Jewish community were most helpful in the development of this study. The collaboration of my research partner, Professor Gene Levine and his associates in UCLA's Sociology Department, was an indispensable aspect of the survey research process. Many of the leading Jewish social scientists and Jewish educators in the country participated in the validation of the Jewish Identity Scale.

A major contributor to the book was Professor Bruce A. Phillips of Hebrew Union College in Los Angeles who read and reread the manuscript and offered creative assistance and encouragement.

I am particularly thankful to Dr. David L. Lieber, president of the University of Judaism, and to Richard S. Volpert, who chaired its Center for Contemporary Jewish Life. Along with the members of the University's Board, they recognized the importance of this project and provided the funding that made it possible. The support of the David E. Sanford Memorial Fund is also gratefully acknowledged.

Dr. David Gordis, executive vice president of the American Jewish Committee, provided vigorous backing from the very inception of this undertaking. Members of the American Jewish Committee staff in New York offered generous advice on the editing of the manuscript.

Dr. Ronald Watt provided valuable assistance through computer programming and analyses of the data. My secretary, Karin Garrity, worked patiently and skillfully toward the preparation of the manuscript. Maryann Elbaum, my talented editor, added the knowledge and polish that greatly improved the final product. To all of those who helped to make this book a reality, I extend my profound appreciation.

Table of Contents

Preface

The decades following World War II saw major demographic changes in the American Jewish community. Among the most dramatic was the migration of tens of thousands of Jews to the West Coast. By the year 1959 there were well over half a million Jews in the western states, with four hundred thousand of them in the greater Los Angeles area. It took only a relatively brief period of time for them to sink their roots into the soil of Southern California and to build major institutions—synagogues, centers, schools of higher learning, day schools, camps—and the central coordinating agencies which are the hallmark of every major Jewish community. Today, Los Angeles is the second largest Jewish population center in the world, which, in its diversity, reflects the totality of American Jewry. All national Jewish organizations are represented in it, as are all of the religious movements, in their varying forms of expression. The Jewish Federation Council of Los Angeles is one of the best of its kind and from its board and other local Jewish groups have emerged men and women who occupy positions of national leadership on the Jewish scene.

While Los Angeles scarcely typifies the rest of the country, it is fair to say that some national trends are often observable here first. This is becoming increasingly true as population shifts continue away from the Northeast into the West and the Sun Belt. That is why students of the contemporary American Jewish scene must pay close attention to what is happening in this very sizeable community and why the present study should be of great interest to them. It is the result of some four years of research by two very competent sociologists, Professors Gene Levine of UCLA and Neil Sandberg of Loyola Marymount University. Dr. Sandberg, who is the author of this book, also has a first hand acquaintance with the Los Angeles Jewish community, having served as the regional director of the American Jewish Committee for over twenty years. It was he who first broached the study to the University of Judaism and designed the questionnaire on which it was based. It was he, also, who saw it through to its successful conclusion and publication.

This valuable book should be of interest not only to sociologists and other scholars, but also to those who are concerned about the future of Jewish life in America. While it tends to support the findings of some recent surveys of the American Jewish condition, it takes issue with others, in each case supporting the author's conclusions with detailed analyses of the data. It concludes with policy recommendations which are well balanced and which deserve careful consideration.

Dr. David L. Lieber, President
University of Judaism, Los Angeles

This is an important book and not just for the Jews of Los Angeles. Informed by relevant sociological studies of the Jews, Dr. Sandberg has added original research and penetrating insight into a complex community which carries within it the seeds of American Jewry's future. Carefully researched and judiciously balanced, it is an invaluable text for Jews, lay and professional, who care about the changing condition and character of American Jewry.

Rabbi Harold M. Schulweis
Valley Beth Shalom, Encino, California

In many ways the City of Los Angeles is a test case for creative Jewish survival in the diaspora. Blessed with a large and active Jewish population and having developed a sophisticated infrastructure of educational, charitable, and communal organizations, the prerequisites for a flowering of Jewish life in Los Angeles appear to be in place. Dr. Sandberg has studied Jewish identity in Los Angeles and in this important work reveals how this great community is doing. The author has broken new ground, developing a Jewish identity scale, and has placed the results of his survey research into the broader context of Jewish life in America. This book is "must" reading, not only for students of Los Angeles Jewish life, but for all who are interested in the prognosis for creative Jewish survival in America.

Dr. David M. Gordis, Executive Vice President
American Jewish Committee, New York

Dr. Sandberg's methodology is sound, the conclusions valid, and as Jewish sociology, this book is important. It addresses three important lacunae in the Jewish sociological literature. First, it is one of all too few studies to address Jewish identity seriously and to place it within the larger theoretical perspective of comparative ethnic identity. Second, it pays particular attention to the emergence of the fourth generation, and thus to the future of American Jewry. Third, although Los Angeles became the second largest Jewish community in the U.S. 30 years ago, this is only the second book and the first sociological study of this community.

Dr. Bruce A. Phillips, Associate Professor
Hebrew Union College, Los Angeles

Dr. Neil C. Sandberg has written this book out of the richness of his experience. He brings to his account of Jewish life in Los Angeles a wisdom enabling him to recognize that, as he says, "there are a dozen different Judaisms with various visions. . . What we have is a sense of community." Dr. Sandberg has fashioned a genuinely impressive statement.

Dr. Uri D. Herscher, Executive Vice President
Hebrew Union College, Los Angeles

One of the Jewish community's most respected professionals has combined an incisive analysis of available studies with his own research and expertise to hold up a mirror for American Jews. It is an invaluable document for all those seeking to add to the blueprint of Jewish survival.

Rabbi Marvin Hier, Dean
Yeshiva University of Los Angeles

Sandberg has written a "must read" book for the understanding of the vibrant, complex, and often misunderstood Jewish community of Los Angeles. He takes us briefly through the origins and history of the community and then presents, through detailed description and solid analysis, a comprehensive picture of patterns of Jewish identity, affiliation, commitments, and problems. His discussions of generational differences, of Los Angeles' New Jews, and of the needs of the young adult population, are at the same time disturbing and challenging. Sandberg does not hesitate to draw conclusions from the extensive surveys he conducted and to suggest a realistic agenda for policy and community planning. The text is provided with extensive charts and statistical analysis, an appendix on methods and procedures, and an excellent bibliography.

Lewis M. Barth, Professor
Hebrew Union College, Los Angeles

An important contribution to the understanding of Jews not only in Los Angeles, but in the United States. Southern California today represents what the country will be tomorrow. Neil Sandberg has, in a very readable fashion, added significantly to the insight and knowledge needed for future planning.

Ted Kanner, Executive Vice President
Jewish Federation Council of Greater Los Angeles

Introduction

Throughout most of its history, the mobile, culturally diverse, tradition-free environment of Los Angeles has been hospitable to the Jewish people. As increasing numbers of Jews have joined the trek to the Sun Belt, the Jewish community of Los Angeles has become one of the most important cultural, religious, and educational centers in Jewish life. Jews have come to Los Angeles from all over the country and the world, so that it now has an extraordinarily varied and representative Jewish population. Today, it has a half million Jewish residents who are served by a network of religious and communal institutions that help to sustain and enrich Jewish experience.

> Los Angeles is clearly the center of Jewish life west of the Rocky Mountains and the second city of American Jewry institutionally as well as in numbers, with branches of all the country-wide Jewish organizations and institutions located within its limits. Because of its distance from the East Coast, it has a greater degree of independence from 'New York' than any other regional center in the United States (Elazar, 1972).

So who are the Jews of Los Angeles? In its largest sense, the Jewish community encompasses all those who were born Jews or who formally converted to Judaism. While involvement in organized Jewish activities is no longer an overarching way of life for many people, Los Angeles Jews are linked by a shared history and a sense of kinship. But there is a growing gap between the organizational life of the community and the majority of Jews within it that is reinforced by a trend toward acculturation, or even assimilation, as opportunities to break away from Judaism have expanded in the modern era.

Being Jewish means different things to individual Jews in Los Angeles; there are religious, ethnic, philanthropic, even gastronomic Jews. But most Jews share a sense of oneness with other Jews in Los Angeles as well as throughout the country and abroad. Jewish needs and interests are in the forefront of their agendas and, despite some erosion, Jews try to take care of their own as they have for centuries.

Jews tend to view their concerns for Jewish life in the context of their contributions to the larger community. They feel a commitment and loyalty to the United States, the country that gave them an opportunity to deepen their roots and raise their children in safety. The concept of helping one's own people while assisting others has long been a central underpining of the Jewish value system. This is evidenced on a continuing basis as young Jews are heavily represented in social work, education, and other people-serving activities.

There is significant Jewish participation in the social, economic, and political systems of Los Angeles, with many Jews counted among the most civic-minded and generous citizens of the community. Jews contribute their time, creativity, and resources to most aspects of civic and social development; and while they are found in the forefront of movements for human rights and social justice, they identify with virtually all currents of American political thought. In seeking freedom, opportunity, and escape from cold climates, Jews have helped to build an exciting and thriving community that often sets the pace for the rest of the country.

Most Jews in Los Angeles tend to be comfortable with their Jewishness, although Judaism occupies a relatively small place in their lives. Some are in search of a Jewish lifestyle in an attempt to remake themselves through various forms of personal expression and self-fulfillment. There is a tendency to mix jogging, feminism, careers, and meditation into individual prescriptions for Jewish identity. A low level of Jewish education and knowledge contrasts sharply with a high level of sophistication and general education as Jewish traditions are adjusted to fit prevailing styles in the modern world.

The changes taking place among the Jews of Los Angeles are, in some respects, a manifestation of the changes occurring in the larger community. Los Angeles is shaping a culture that is in the process of blending many world cultures. It is a terminal for Asians, Hispanics, and others seeking political freedom, economic opportunity, and new ways of living. At the same time, Los Angeles has a growing indigenous population reflected in the large number of young people who are native sons and daughters.

In the past, Los Angelenos have been very defensive in explaining their community and its customs to easterners who saw it as "Lotusland," a place for weirdos, cults, and Disneyland fantasies. Today, they are more relaxed and somewhat indifferent to the views of those who deprecate Los Angeles as they try to understand and explain it.

Among its many assets, Los Angeles is the center of a new and popular culture that dictates how people live elsewhere. The impact of the movies developed largely by Jewish writers, directors, and moguls was central in shaping the image of middle class life so pervasive in America. The leadership of Los Angeles, so active in forming national tastes and styles, has been reinforced by the infusion of enormous talent in the various creative arts, along with the business, scientific, and educational elites who continue to move here.

On the down side, the very physical size of Los Angeles means it is very difficult to develop a sense of community. There is no one location to which people go because it is spread out over a huge area, so that Los Angeles has become a number of distinctive subcommunities that take on the character of the entire nation. It is different and the same and, in in many respects, it is a seamless place tied to other centers of American experience and culture.

As Los Angeles has been altered, so has its Jewish population, and the process is far from complete. In terms of the indicators normally used to measure the health of the Jewish community—affiliation, observance, and other traditional behaviors—the problems are serious and increasing. Jews have moved away dramatically from their religious and secular institutions and have abandoned many of the Jewish neighborhoods that provided a framework for the processes of Jewish socialization. These factors and others point to the existence of major difficulties that challenge the continuity of the Jewish community and the possibilities for its meaningful future (Lieber, 1977).

The disaffiliation of increasing numbers of Jews has led Jewish leaders and scholars to feel that a greater understanding of Jewish identity and behavior can help in dealing more effectively with the complexities of Jewish life. This study is intended to provide a useful data base for those in the organized Jewish community who make difficult decisions that involve spending millions of dollars to achieve religious and communal objectives. It is hoped that a broad assessment of the Los Angeles Jewish population will contribute to the shaping of new policies and programs that lead to a more open and inclusive outreach to those not presently linked to Jewish institutions.

To this end, the Center for the Study of Contemporary Jewish Life, University of Judaism, launched the first comprehensive study of the attitudes and behavior of the adult Jewish population in greater Los Angeles. One of the goals was to determine by means of a household survey, the correlates of differential degrees of Jewish identity as measured by a set of identity scales especially developed for the study. Another key objective was to discover the factors that make for or inhibit participation in the organized Jewish community. An advisory committee was established by the University to assist in the organization and development of the research process, as well as to provide quantitative and qualitative input and guidance that would help to assure the success of the venture.

Following the validation of the identity scales by a nationwide panel of experts, other questions were prepared covering a wide range of Jewish attitudinal and behavioral variables. A group of UCLA students participated in a pretest; an interviewers field manual was prepared; a randomized sampling frame was constructed covering the Los Angeles Metropolitan Area; and a canvas of 5,000 homes was conducted (see Appendix).

Cross-tabulations of the responses were developed using the Chi-square (x^2) test to determine levels of significance. For purposes of this study, the .05, .01 and.001 levels were utilized as standards for assessing probability distribution. Some of the key variables were examined from different vantage points, and references to such items as affiliation, mobility, Jewish education, Israel, and intermarriage appear in different chapters.

Over the years efforts have been made to measure Jewish identity and identification using various attitudinal and behavioral indicators. Synagogue membership and attendance as well as observance of ritual behavior have been among the primary characteristics used as determinants of Jewish behavior. Attitudinal studies have assessed feelings about Israel, other Jews, Jewish neighborhoods, and concern about anti-Semitism. Communal participation and responsibility toward other Jews have been examined along with exogamous marriage and other forms of self-exclusion from the Jewish group. Recent studies have attempted to assess the relative influence of Jewish institutions and experiences on Jewish identification. They have looked at parents, spouses, friends, Jewish education, demographic characteristics such as generation, age, sex, and social class as well as different points in the life cycle. A widespread assumption has been the view that no satisfactory Jewish identity scale exists that is both valid and reliable. Consequently, various attitudinal and behavioral characteristics have been utilized in this study as measures of Jewish identity.

In the last two or three decades, demographers have conducted national Jewish population surveys and a number of community studies. The data gathered show a clear process of Jewish cultural attrition from generation to generation as a result of erosive factors in the general environment and the deficiencies of the home. At the same time, selected indicators point to a leveling off in the decline of Jewish identification and some upturn in Jewish belief and commitment. The findings are similar to a number of those developed in this study and, despite significant variations, suggest that patterns of Jewish thought and behavior in Los Angeles are often comparable to those of the American Jewish population.

The American Jewish Committee pioneered much of the research in the 1950s through questions that asked people to define who was a good Jew. The leading qualities of the good Jew were seen as ethical behavior, humanitarianism, and civic spirit, and little difference was found between the good Jew and the good person (American Jewish Committee, 1959). A later study conceptualized Jewish identity differently in terms of a willing awareness of belonging to the group and accepting its values, standards, and traditions (American Jewish Committee, 1963). Lazerwitz (1967), however, saw the dominant variables in contemporary Jewish identification as generations in this country, family life cycle, religious behavior, and activity in Jewish organizations.

Another study initiated by the American Jewish Committee was of the "Lakeville" Jewish community that was, to some degree, similar to the suburban milieu of Los Angeles Jewry. Sklare and Greenblum (1967) reported that the American environment tends to inhibit the development of conditions for the creation of a strong Jewish identity since the majority culture dominates. This is a particular problem for third generation American Jews who are not rebelling against their Jewishness but who have little Jewish content in their lives. While the decline of traditional Jewish thought and practice has been arrested, "Lakeville" Jews are submerged in a dominant culture that contributes to their Jewish sensitivity and facilitates varying degrees of acculturation. Still, most of their close friends are other Jews, and a significant proportion plan some formal Jewish education for their children including bar mitzvah and confirmation.

Studies of Providence Jewry (Goldstein and Goldscheider, 1968), the Jews in St. Paul (Dashefsky and Shapiro, 1974), and Los Angeles Jews (Massaryk, 1968) also found sharp generational declines in traditional ritual practices. Using data from the National Jewish Population Study, Himmelfarb and Loar (1984) suggest that Jewish identification declines with generational distance from the immigrant group, but that some stabilization develops by the fourth generation especially among the Orthodox. Waxman (1981) observes that the indicators of Jewishness show a decline in each succeeding generation, but sees some evidence of a reversal in the fourth generation. The third generation may well be experiencing some of the conflicts of the second as they anticipated but did not achieve full acceptance in American culture. But the fourth generation has had the time and leisure for self-exploration which is leading many toward a return to some of the values and norms of the immigrant generation. Within the fourth generation, however, there are contrasting trends rather than a single directional trend.

In his 1981 national survey of American Jews, Cohen (1983) points to a sharp decline in observance of stringent rituals such as observing kashruth and lighting Sabbath candles, but Passover seder attendance is very high, followed by lighting Chanukah candles and fasting on Yom Kippur. Membership in congregations and Jewish organizations is considerably higher nationally than in Los Angeles, but other characteristics are comparable such as the high proportion of close Jewish friends as well as cultural and political behaviors.

While there are similarities in generational patterns evidenced in the 1975 Boston study (Cohen, 1983), the 1981 survey conducted in New York (Ritterband and Cohen, 1984), and the current Los Angeles analysis, an important difference emerges regarding exogamous marriages. The incidence of intermarriage for Los Angeles Jews is substantially higher in the third and fourth generations than in New York and Boston, and Los Angeles intermarriage rates are also greater than those of Philadelphia (Yancey and Goldstein, 1984). Studies of Jewish populations in St. Louis (Tobin, 1982), Milwaukee (Phillips and Weinberg, 1984), and Denver (Phillips and Judd, 1981) also reflect the sharply rising incidence of intermarriage among Jews in the midwestern and western parts of the country.

The responses to the various studies indicate an extensive psychic attachment to Israel both in terms of political support and personal visits. The data also indicate that a significant proportion of Jews living in Denver, New York, Milwaukee, Phoenix, Los Angeles, and elsewhere have very low incomes, with those who are economically distressed distributed through all age groups and less able to participate in the life of the organized Jewish community (Bayer, 1983). And, as in Los Angeles, there is a widespread belief among Jews that anti-Semitism is an ongoing problem (Cohen, 1983 and Phillips,1984).

The growing movement of Jews to the West is reflected in the formation of new Jewish households among single persons never married, the widowed, and divorced with a consequent reduction in the number of young children living at home. In places like St. Louis, Jews are using their community institutions and networks as a basis for patterns of belonging rather than forming high-density Jewish neighborhoods (Tobin, 1982). At the same time, the reports from New York, Milwaukee, and other places point to the maintenance of some stable neighborhoods, with many feeling that living among other Jews is important to them. In aggregate, the studies of Jewish populations across the country, including Los Angeles, indicate some decline in Jewish attitudes and behaviors, with various indicators pointing to a considerable residue of Jewishness as well as new signs of Jewish vitality.

Young educated Jews in Los Angeles represent an important resource for the Jewish community. Although many are not connected to Jewish organizations, they tend to be highly committed and express very positive feelings about their aspirations for a Jewish future for themselves and their children. A Jewish renaissance is taking place among fourth generation Los Angeles Jews who, on a number of indicators, are more Jewishly sensitive and concerned than those of the third generation.

Israel is the most powerful indicator of Jewish identity today, and while most Los Angeles Jews are not Zionists and have never been to Israel, they are deeply committed to its security and well-being. The question of Israel's survival is of profound concern to nearly all Jews, and there is little difference between the affiliated and unaffiliated regarding support for Israel even in the event of a policy conflict with the United States. Most see Israel as a spiritual and cultural center as well as a place where Jews can decide their own destiny. Concern for the survival of the Jewish people goes beyond Israel to encompass Soviet Jewry and the condition of all Jews here and abroad.

Fewer than half of the Jews of Los Angeles are affiliated with any religious or Jewish group nor do they contribute to Jewish institutions. The affiliated and unaffiliated can be distinguished in a variety of ways in terms of their Jewish attitudes and behaviors. The affiliated tend to express themselves consistently in a manner that displays their Jewish commitment. But the unaffiliated also reflect a considerable awareness of and concern with a number of Jewish issues and, in some respects, there is relatively little difference between them.

There are constituencies that are underrepresented in the organized Jewish community—young people, singles, women, the poor, seniors, the divorced, and widowed. Those who have the greatest problems are the least involved, and they lack power and influence in Jewish institutional life. Although Jewish organizations want their participation, the methods they use are sometimes ineffectual and counterproductive. The trend in organized Jewish life is toward centralism of power and decision making, and this frequently cuts off opportunities for large numbers of individuals to become part of the institutional community. There tends to be an unwillingness to share power, a sense of elitism, and a feeling that a select few should decide what is best for Jews as a people.

Los Angeles Jews are today defining themselves far more in ethnic and cultural terms than as members of a religious group, and many regular observances and traditional practices have declined substantially. Some deeply religious Jews find their spiritual satisfaction outside the synagogue because they do not feel the unique wisdom of Judaism is presented in ways that have meaning for them. Another factor that inhibits involvement in congregations is the high cost of participation, with a significant number of Los Angeles Jews feeling that synagogue membership is too expensive.

At the same time, the need for community in a fragmented, alienated society motivates many to affirm their religious identity. The decline of traditional Judaism was reversed in the decade after the Six-Day War with youthful and vigorous participation giving it new vitality. This was in some respects a reaction to the counterculture of the 1960s. It was also a consequence of the infusion of renewed enthusiasm into Los Angeles Jewish life by such groups as the Hasidim who, along with Orthodox, Conservative, and Reform Jews, are providing a new kind of authenticity to Judaism by offering tradition in a community environment.

The huge Jewish migration to Los Angeles and continuing mobility within the metropolitan area have contributed to a loss of close-knit and supportive relationships that, in the past, provided social and psychological support for the individual. Family, friends, and neighborhood institutions are less available, and newcomers to Los Angeles frequently find themselves lacking the assistance they need to adjust to new circumstances. Uprooting and resettlement tend to create anxiety, tension, and stress within the family unit, and endanger the capacity to sustain human relationships and social cohesion. The loss of community has diminished a sense of belonging and security for many Jews whose inability to cope with their condition has made them casualties of an impersonal and sometimes threatening society.

Still, there are strong and continuing patterns of Jewish association in the social, economic, and communal environments, and Los Angeles Jews report that most of their closest friends are other Jews. Many who no longer live in Jewish areas are more comfortable with other Jews and they yearn for a Jewish neighborhood which is seen as a friendlier place to live. Together with strong economic and communal ties, the primary networks of family and personal companions continue to be central to the ways in which Jews maintain supportive contacts and linkages.

As a newer and less stratified community, Los Angeles Jews developed a differentiated and diffuse suburban lifestyle long before many of the other Jewish communities in the United States. They have left the traditional urban, Orthodox community that provided the daily reinforcement of Jewish institutional systems and face-to-face association, and increasingly live in the psychological enclaves of suburbia where non-Jewish influences tend to be more pervasive. This has led to a process of social change and adjustment in which Jewish identity has declined, but still remains a significant factor in the lives of most people. The bond of identity continues to be expressed through formal and informal structural associations and is maintained by a common history and tradition. It is also supported by the currently fashionable voicing of ethnic identification and pride, as well as by the emergence of a new militancy resulting from the emerging needs of group self-interest and the abrasiveness of intergroup contacts and perceptions.

The terrors of the Holocaust contributed to a rise in Jewish consciousness among Los Angeles Jews that reinforced the need for mutual aid and togetherness. This concern for unity and self-defense was further stimulated by the Six-Day War and the Yom Kippur War as Jews committed themselves in psychological, economic, and political ways to the determination that "never again" would they allow their fate to be determined by others.

The current assertiveness of many Jews here and throughout the country has been defined as "Jewish survivalism," a phenomenon grounded in the belief that Jews must assure the future of Judaism by taking control of their own destiny. Attacks against Israel, anti-Semitism, and Jewish apathy are challenged by the determination to build a new Jewish civilization steeped in the tragic lessons of Jewish powerlessness that characterized the Holocaust. Jewish identification is often reflected in a new civil religion that focuses on the social, economic, and ethnic interests of the group.

There is increasing activism in Los Angeles Jewish life with many anxious to use the political process, demonstrations, and other pressures to attain group objectives. Jews are very concerned with extremism and the threat it poses to the democratic process. Nonetheless, a majority are willing to prevent the expression of anti-Semitic views by Nazi-type groups, even when such measures challenge the historic commitment of Jews to civil liberties and First Amendment rights. The political orientation of Los Angeles Jewry has shifted considerably from the liberal-left to a more liberal-moderate stance, and Jews have virtually abandoned the radical and collectivist views held by some in the past.

There is a contradiction between the ways in which Jews and

non-Jews view the presence of anti-Semitism in this country. A 1981 Harris Poll indicates non-Jewish Americans feel strongly that Jews are no longer victims of discrimination, but the perceptions of Los Angeles Jews are quite different with a high proportion reporting they have felt some anti-Semitism. Better educated Jews have had the most anti-Semitic exposure, perhaps because they are more mobile and have had greater contact with non-Jews. Considerable discrimination is noted in business and employment and even more in private clubs. Younger Jews report far less experience with anti-Semitism although they manifest a high level of anxiety about exposing their Jewishness in public.

While Jews are increasingly focused on issues of self-interest, there is continued support for helping the poor and minorities, strong identification with human rights issues and ongoing concern for social reform consistent with civic stability. The Jewish right-winger is usually a moderate by the standards of anyone else. Moreover, the social commitment of Jews carries over strongly into the civic world with a substantial majority claiming to give money to non-Jewish causes.

Intermarriage among Jews in Los Angeles has increased dramatically in recent years stimulated, in part, by early association with non-Jews including a considerable degree of interdating. This has been accompanied by a substantial lessening of resistance and even a growing receptivity among most Jews to both interdating and the prospective intermarriage of their children. Many of the non-Jewish spouses have converted to Judaism, while few Jews have converted to their spouse's religion, pointing to a considerable net gain of Jewish adherents. At the same time, some younger Jews are beginning to express concern about the implications of intermarriage for themselves and the future of Jewish life.

The demographic problems stemming from intermarriage are reinforced by a considerably lower birthrate among Jews which has reached the point where they reproduce less than any other American group and are not replacing themselves. The issue is compounded by the emergence of higher divorce rates, more single parent families, and the changing behavior of young men and women reflected in fewer marriages and the growth of alternate life styles. With the Jewish family under severe stress, its capacity to effectively transmit the values and beliefs of Judaism is increasingly in doubt.

The Jewish community of Los Angeles is in a constant state of flux with people and institutions moving to meet personal and communal needs. Jews have developed a complex organizational culture in order to assure their physical, communal, and religious survival. A good deal of what is done under the auspices of Jewish organizations is philanthropic and, to a great extent, the institutions themselves have become the "culture" of many Jews. This activity is reinforced by the sense of mutual responsibility developed in the many lands where Jews faced persecution and oppression.

No single body represents all Jewish interests, although the Jewish Federation Council of Greater Los Angeles comes closest to being an umbrella group. Yet even the Federation is not a monolithic entity and the more than five hundred organizations and numerous committees that are part of its structure represent a loosely knit, broadly diverse and sometimes competitive system.

There are differing points of view in Los Angeles Jewish life, especially on the question of who speaks for the Jews. Some would like it to be the Federation and others look to such groups as the Anti-Defamation League of B'nai B'rith or the American Jewish Committee. But most Jews challenge the notion that anyone speaks for them. They may like the idea of working through organizations to achieve specific goals, but the majority prefer to speak for themselves.

The Federation plays a dominant role in community fund raising and decision making, but social, cultural, historical, and economic factors also affect patterns of communication and decisions are often determined by who knows whom in the friendship and acquaintenceship systems. Decision making is usually based on voluntary participation but it is not necessarily democratic. The struggle for governance is sometimes influenced by those whose fund raising capabilities give them special leverage in the Jewish communal system. Moreover, there tends to be conflict between those who seek to centralize power and others who opt for a diverse and more pluralistic community.

Today, the Federation encompasses a number of new geographic areas in order to provide services and raise funds, assisted by a large professional staff and a number of lay leaders who help to administer a variety of local, national, and overseas programs. Aid is provided for Israel, the Jewish poor, and other social welfare and educational needs, but some of the important Jewish organizations carry on their own programs and fund raising, often independent of the Federation system. Campaigns are conducted for Jewish higher education, universities in Israel, Jewish hospitals, synagogues, and community relations programs, so that fund raising has become the major activity of the organized Jewish community.

But there is much more to Jewish life than fund raising, and hundreds of different groups contribute to a complex and creative community. Activated by a core of committed people, these groups offer programs spanning welfare, religion, education, culture, and the needs of Jews abroad. Among them are agencies seeking to assist the low-income elderly, the growing group of single parents living on marginal incomes, the resettlement of new immigrants, health and psychiatric care, and other social service enterprises.

Efforts to deal with the needs of the Jewish poor are sometimes frustrated by the "myth of universal Jewish affluence." But agencies of the Federation and others are engaged in a systematic outreach to the sick, the poor, the aged, and single parent families. Trained volunteers and staff provide guidance and aid in storefront operations on Fairfax and in the San Fernando Valley, and mobile units are available to those who live in areas lacking Jewish communal agencies. Thus, some of the unaffiliated are tied to the Jewish community in a kind of symbiotic relationship by receiving services and aid from Jewish programs dealing with recreation, culture, nutrition, and health.

There is a strong commitment to Jewish education among most Jews in Los Angeles who believe it is important for their children and to a Jewish future. This attitude is evident even among those who, themselves, have had very little Jewish education, come from non-religious backgrounds, or are intermarried. Those who get considerable schooling are a self-selected group who are more Jewishly identified in the first place, but it is interesting that individuals with only a moderate Jewish education are the most likely to give financial support to Jewish causes.

Jewish education is an important element in the formation of Jewish identity, and we are witnessing a rise in adult Jewish education, more and more college students participating in Jewish studies programs, and increasing numbers of summer camps integrating Jewish content and recreation. The commitment to Jewish life and learning is greatly strengthened by the University of Judaism, Hebrew Union College, Yeshiva University, and a number of Jewish libraries.

The Jewish day school movement is also growing with thousands of youngsters now enrolled at the elementary and secondary levels and in preschools. Jewish education is slowly changing from the shtetl orientation of Eastern Europe to a more American sense of relevancy and a focus on the relationship of diaspora Jews to Israel. Yet, while Israel is central to Jewish consciousness, there is a growing recognition that it does not substitute for an indigenous Jewish identity.

Jews are heavily involved in the intellectual, cultural, and professional life of Los Angeles. There are large numbers of Jewish professors in nearly all of the colleges and universities, and Jews are prominent in the physical and social sciences, literature, law, and medicine. Jewish artists and musicians are in abundance and Jews are strongly represented in the book reading public.

Some Jews participate in Yiddish-speaking cultural clubs and other secular Jewish activities, believing it is possible to be Jewish without adhering to the Jewish religion by reflecting the humanist values of the Jewish experience and an identification with Israel. There are independent secularist shuln, schools where children learn the significance of Jewish holidays, Yiddish, and other aspects of a Jewish heritage. Various less formal groupings of students, intellectuals, and activists also seek to find new ways to express their Jewishness. And on the high holy days, there are makeshift services that spring up in movie theaters and auditoriums to serve the unaffiliated who want to pray on Rosh Hashana and Yom Kippur.

As the Los Angeles Jewish community is separated by time from its immigrant origins, it has, for better or worse, developed more and more of a sense of "normalcy." Jews made the transition from the ghettos of Europe to the full citizenship of America, with many ceasing to be observant as they moved into secular society. They also acquired a full share of the difficulties of modern life including delinquency, alcoholism, divorce, and other social pathologies rooted in the changing lifestyles of American culture.

The processes of assimilation and acculturation are still operative, and Jews in the Los Angeles metropolitan area tend to be less Jewishly involved over time. While many of the children, grandchildren, and great-grandchildren of Jewish immigrants take a substantial interest in the culture and tradition of their forebears, some erosion of Jewish identity has taken place as a consequence of the pressures of Anglo-conformity and because of new patterns of living. The much-discussed resurgence of ethnic interest among Jews is, in part, an expression of a marginal ethnicity altered to meet the requirements of the larger culture.

The dilemma of these analyses is that both negative and positive indicators have been identified in the assessment of Jewish identity, affiliation, and other areas of importance to the future of the Jewish community. There is the good news-bad news dichotomy and the conclusions often depend on how the data are read. The reality is that things are not as bad as they seem, nor are they as good as they could be. There is a need for concern, but not despair, because Los Angeles Jews have built a network of Jewish religious, educational, and helping organizations that is the envy of other groups. Jewish institutions are increasingly focused on questions that relate to Jewish identity and values, and this impacts in very positive ways on the health and strength of the Jewish family.

With all of their problems, Los Angeles Jews are held together by their common memories, history, religion, and the struggle against persecution. They are no longer content to place their fate in the hands of others and have developed an organizational culture that strengthens self-reliance and cuts across ideologies and socio-economic background. Above all, Jews are linked by the feeling that being Jewish has meaning and purpose.

Perhaps the most visible form of "passive" Jewish identification is placing a mezuzah on the door frame of a dwelling. Half of Los Angeles Jewry report having a mezuzah on their door frames, with the affiliated more likely to display one, especially in the fourth generation where 69.2% do so. Among fourth generation, high socioeconomic status Jews, 64.7% of the affiliated and 35.9% of the unaffiliated place a mezuzah on their door frames. These various "passive" behaviors appear to be the minimum acceptable level of Jewish identification for large numbers of unaffiliated Jews.

The more generations Los Angeles Jews are removed from their immigrant ancestors, the weaker their religious identity tends to be. However, this decline in identity is not completely transferred to the area of affiliation. Following a drop in the combined rate of religious and communal affiliation from the second to the third generations, there is a rejuvenation in the fourth generation among the great-grandchildren of the immigrants (see Tables 18 and 43). An examination of age categories shows Los Angeles Jews fifty years of age or over much more likely to be affiliated with a congregation and/or a Jewish communal group than those who are younger (see Table 19), but an assessment of synagogue affiliation alone indicates a decline among those age sixty-five or older (Huberman 1984).

TABLE 18

AFFILIATION (INDEX), BY GENERATION

	Generation			
Affiliated	[illegible]	[illegible]	[illegible]	[illegible]
Yes	[illegible]	58.2	35.1	[illegible]
No	[illegible]	41.8	64.9	52.8
	100.0%	100.0%	100.0%	100.0%

$p < .01$

Section 1

From Past to Present

Introduction to Section 1

Jews in Los Angeles and elsewhere have entered a profound new era marked by an abrupt and radical break with the past. Jewish traditions were already being reshaped when the immigration to this country took place, and Jews broke out of their isolation with a suddenness that challenged their rootedness in the past. Opportunities in the modern secular world opened up possibilities for personal equality and development as well as new forms of Jewish self-expression, organization, and adaptation. While Jewish history taught Jews how to survive in a hostile environment, it did not prepare them to cope with a benevolent one that seeks to absorb them. This is one of the great challenges of American Jewish life.

The Jewish experience in America has demonstrated that Judaism can develop in an open and plural society and that the interplay of various cultures does not prevent the preservation of Jewish communal expression.The social contract with America has been rewritten from a commitment to give up ethnicity in order to facilitate entry into American culture to the current acceptance and encouragement of ethnic feelings as an aspect of American identity. Jews are now free to be Jewish in a new way as an act of personal choice rather than imposition. They are able to adopt the notion that peoplehood connects Jews everywhere, while they participate fully and freely in American life.

The problems of Jewish adjustment have been underscored by rapid increases in the population and major shifts in geographic distribution. This was accompanied by very significant adjustments in social, economic, and educational patterns as Jews became increasingly middle class and urban, taking opportunities afforded by liberal, democratic institutions and the expansion of industry and commerce. The transformation of the occupational and social structures of the Jewish community corresponded to the development of modern secular education and urban vocations and was paralleled by a declining birthrate, an increase of intermarriage, and assimilation.

The loss of six million people during the Nazi Holocaust was a demographic catastrophe from which Jews have still not recovered, and there are now only thirteen million Jews in the world with more than three million residing in Israel and the remainder in the diaspora (American Jewish Yearbook, 1985). Today, the Jewish population of the United States is estimated at 5,817,000, which indicates a modest decline from the figure of 5,860,900 for 1979. Within the Pacific region, however, the Jewish population has expanded from 3.2% in 1900, to 3.6% in 1930, 12.2% in 1968 (Goldstein, 1981), and 14.3% in 1984 (American Jewish Yearbook, 1985). The growth of the western Jewish population has been more rapid than that of the general population as Jews increasingly concentrate in the professions and other occupations marked by high mobility.

Jews in the diaspora have fertility and birth rates that are far lower than those of other groups in the population, with mixed and late marriages tending to reduce these levels even further. The fertility rate of American Jews has declined from 3.7 children per family in the mid-1940s to under 1.5 children in the period from 1967 to 1971 (Johnson, 1976 and Schmelz, 1981). This means that the birth rate for Jews in the United States is lower than the 2.4 average number of births per woman for the total white group and the 2.1 figure believed to be needed for replacement (Goldstein, 1981 and Waxman, 1981).

Some social scientists are predicting that the Jewish population in the United States will decline dramatically in the years ahead, and one prognosticator even suggests that in the year 2076 there will only be 944,000 Jews at most and, perhaps, as few as 10,410 (Bergman, 1977). This appears to be a grossly pessimistic prediction, and others feel the Jewish population will remain relatively stable to the year 2000 and then be reduced by one to two million over the next few generations (Goldstein, 1981).

Many Jews over thirty-five have lost contact with their childhood friends and hometowns, have attended more than one university, and have moved to seek better job opportunities. Their new friends are often other alienated, poorly Jewish-educated and lonely persons. Children no longer know the excitement of the extended family and those who have left home often do not write or visit their relatives (Burnham, 1980). Moreover, new migrants to a community are much less active in communal structures than are long time residents (Sandberg, 1978 and Zimmer, 1955), and the emerging pattern is one of great dispersion and general integration into the larger population.

A new Jewish generation is growing up without the visceral

sense of Jewishness of the past that was gained from personal interaction and face-to-face association. Large numbers of Jews live in mixed neighborhoods as they seek some measure of social integration and association in terms of their living patterns. Jews needed a substitute for Jewish neighbors and built synagogues and community centers. This did not represent a religious revival because many utilized the synagogue as a symbol through which they could express their identity without significant participation in its activities (Gans, 1979). But Etzioni (1959) noted that ethnic groups could maintain themselves in the psychological enclaves of suburbia through communication, limited social situations, and core institutions.

Although the Jewish family has also been undergoing substantial changes, it is still one of the most important structures for the transmission of Jewish identity and continuity. But the Jewish family is in difficulty with new household configurations including the two-career family that sometimes deprives children of adequate parental care along with a denigration of the role and status of mothers and homemakers. The growing enrollment of women in graduate work and in developing independent careers often means delaying or not having any children. All of this has been accompanied by a decline in religious beliefs and practice along with a deemphasis of the work ethic and a growth in the pursuit of self-gratification.

The Jewish friendship group is an important element that works to preserve Jewish group identity, and most Jews spend more time with friends than with relatives. The tendency to homogenous Jewish friendships becomes strong in late adolescence as relationships with other Jews strengthen feelings of ethnic solidarity. Some are not comfortable in the presence of non-Jews and Jewish social networks are highly prevalent even among those uninvolved in synagogue life. Up to 60% of the unobservant claim that all their close friends are Jewish or are Gentiles married to Jews as compared to 70% of the most observant (Sklare and Greenblum, 1967).

On most indicators, Jews have become a highly successful socioeconomic group. They have moved significantly into managerial and professional categories and there are new signs of an upturn in entrepreneurship. But the Jewish poor have been somewhat neglected by the Jewish community and in public programs, and it was only in the early 1970s that they attracted serious attention

(American Jewish Committee, 1973). What we are witnessing is the relative financial success of a considerable segment of the Jewish population which, when factored into aggregate statistics, tends to mask the continuing problems of large numbers of Jews who are at the lower rungs of the economic ladder.

A National Opinion Research Center study found Jews the best educated Americans with 14 average years of education as compared with 13.5 for Episcopalians, 12.7 for Presbyterians, 11.9 for Methodists, and 11.5 for Catholics (Greeley, 1974). More than 80% of Jewish youth attend college underscoring the high value Jewish men and women place on educational attainment; the college attendance figure for non-Jewish youth is only about 40% (Newsweek, March 1, 1971). Jews have the highest percentage of college graduates with over one-third having achieved this level of education (Greeley, 1974). But there is a drop of 25% in the proportion of Jewish freshmen in all colleges from 4.2% in 1970 to 3.2% in 1980. This reflects the decline in the number of Jewish eighteen year olds brought about by lower Jewish birth rates (Drew, 1981).

A serious concern among Jews is that their median age is now forty-nine, making them one of the oldest of the various American subgroups (Cohen, 1982). Generational status also has relevance to the future as more and more Jews are American born and there is less outside reinforcement from immigration. Most studies show the percentage of American born Jews above 70% (Goldstein and Goldscheider, 1968) and becoming as high as 90% (Cohen, 1982). The National Jewish Population Study found 23% of households foreign born and about 20% third generation or more (Massarik and Chenkin, 1973). This is changing significantly with the proportions of third and fourth generation Jews growing rapidly.

A number of studies indicate that the less religious the Jewish home, the greater the chances of both intermarriage and the loss of Jewish identity (Lazerwitz and Harrison, 1979 and Massarik and Chenkin, 1973). While Jews are more resistant to intermarriage than Catholics or Protestants and less willing to convert to the faiths of their spouses, they are accepting intermarriage more readily than they did in the past (Mayer, 1985). The level of intermarriage rose from 2% of those who had married between 1900 and 1920, to 6% married between 1940 and 1960, 17% of the 1960-65 group, and 32% of those marrying in the previous five years (Massarik and

Chenkin, 1973). The problem has continued to grow, and there are forecasts of even higher intermarriage rates for the future (Massarik, 1973).

A significant proportion of non-Jewish spouses convert to Judaism, and some who do not convert identify as Jews and raise their children as Jews. Many Jewish parents now feel that intermarriage does not inevitably lead to assimilation and hope that the non-Jewish spouses of their children will either convert to Judaism or raise their grandchildren as Jews. The increasingly relaxed attitudes of parents are reinforced by their commitment to universalism and equality, so that the opposition of some Jews to intermarriage runs counter to the principles by which they raise their children.

As Jews leave their families, friends, and neighborhoods to pursue careers in the modern world, the cohesiveness of the Jewish community is weakened. It becomes more and more difficult to maintain the traditional family and to hold on to the spiritual and cultural values of Jewish life. There are social and psychological costs associated with mobility, and interpersonal and communal ties are disrupted. In spite of the problems inherent in this process, however, Jews feel a deep sense of rootedness and belongingness in both American and Jewish culture. The Americanization of Jews and Judaism continues as each Jew finds for himself the "precise calibrations by which he can maintain the fine balance between living in the general society and living as a Jew" (Dawidowicz, 1982).

I

Historical Development

The history of the Jews in Los Angeles was linked to the history of the entire population, as Jews and non-Jews alike faced similar problems and possibilities in the evolution of a pioneering community. Regional attributes and obstacles influenced the attitudes and behavior of Los Angelenos in all periods of its development in what came to be an increasingly interrelated future. There were similar opportunities for involvement in the growth of the social, economic, and political milieu in a place that was not constrained by the rigid historical and cultural patterns of the society.

From the beginning, Los Angeles attracted Jews who were escaping the long history of anti-Semitism and persecution in Europe and other places. Sometimes they settled in other cities before moving on to the West but, once they arrived in Los Angeles, they were here to stay and few emigrated back to their countries of origin. Their lives were intertwined with the expansion and development of the region in opening up the frontier and pioneering in business, science, and the arts. It was a complex process in which the immigrant culture was separated from its old-world traditions and the children of the immigrants were separated from the immigrant culture.

In the earliest history of Los Angeles, there were several Indian villages whose population subsisted by hunting and fishing rather than through growing crops. These first inhabitants were isolated by mountains and deserts, and developed an insular society that tended to be conservative in outlook. Their culture was invaded and taken over by the Spanish occupation and, over the years, the early Indian culture virtually disappeared.

Los Angeles was founded by the Spaniards in 1781 as one of a series of coastal pueblos that complemented California's presidios and missions. The community was named El Pueblo de Nuestra Senora la Reina de Los Angeles—the Town of Our Lady the Queen of the Angels. It continued for many years under Spanish and then Mexican rule as a small town comprised of Spanish, Indian, black, and racially mixed populations.

In the late sixteenth and early seventeenth centuries an unknown number of Spanish and Portugese Jews, concealing their identity to elude the Mexican Colonial Inquisition, helped establish Spanish settlements in what is now the American Southwest (Rochlin, 1984). Jews from other places were emigrating to California in the 1820s and 1830s seeking to develop the empty territories along with non-Jews. In 1848, as a result of the Mexican war, California became a part of the United States and it was ratified as a State of the Union in 1850.

The gold rush of 1848 contributed greatly to the development of California and, when Los Angeles was incorporated as a city in 1850, there were nearly two thousand residents including eight individuals believed to be Jewish. One of them, Jacob Frankfort, came to Los Angeles as part of the Rowland-Workman party that arrived on December 12, 1841. In a census taken in 1851, his presence was noted in Los Angeles as living in a place called Bell's Row, at the corner of Aliso and Los Angeles Streets, along with seven other unmarried Jewish merchants from Germany.

These Jews were soon joined by a number of others from Germany, Bohemia, and Hungary who were seeking to escape oppression and to find political and economic opportunity. There were also a number of Polish Jews who emigrated to California in the nineteenth century, some of whom contributed greatly to the development of Los Angeles. In the early days, there was considerable social separation according to national origin and those of East European descent often found themselves at the lower end of the social scale.

While most Jews settled in the Northeast and Middle West, many were drawn by the growth of California, and a group of Jewish immigrants landed in San Francisco in 1849 (Narell, 1982). By 1860 the California Jewish population was estimated at ten thousand, with a heavy concentration in San Francisco but only one hundred living in Los Angeles (I.J. Benjamin, 1956). A Jew named Morris Goodman came to Los Angeles in 1849 and, when Los Angeles was incorporated as a city in 1850, he was elected to its first City Council. In order to combat lawlessness, he helped to establish its police department and another Jew, Emil Harris, was appointed Chief of Police in 1877.

There was a further influx of pioneering Jews, including Isaias W. Hellman who came to Los Angeles in 1859. After working for years as a clerk, then starting a bank and going into real estate, he moved to San Francisco where he became one of the founders of what is today known as the Wells Fargo Bank. Jewish women also contributed substantially to the opening up of the community, and Los Angeles history is replete with their accomplishments. Among them was Ernestine Greenebaum who was one of the first Jewish women to come to Los Angeles, and who in the 1870s opened the White House Hotel that catered to unmarried immigrants.

From the start, Jews were well accepted and represented an important part of the communal and economic life of Los Angeles. The family of Harris Newmark was enormously influential in the early development of the community in its business, civic, and political affairs. They were active in commerce, banking, and land development, and some of the family pioneered in the professions. Newmark arrived in Los Angeles in 1853 and, a year later, others in the family also came to settle. They soon became part of the communal establishment and, starting in 1862, members of the family served in various public positions including city attorney, city council, county treasurer, county supervisor, school board, and city clerk.

Jews participated in the cultural and volunteer activities of the community throughout the more than one hundred years of Jewish life in Los Angeles. From the start, they were involved significantly in such groups as the Masons, the Odd Fellows, and various charitable groups. In 1880, I.W. Hellman contributed part of the land that made possible the establishment of the University of Southern California, a Methodist school that was the first institution of higher learning in Southern California (Dumke, 1944). Jews helped to found the Chamber of Commerce, the Board of Trade, the Library Association, and Associated Charities, and they were among the first members of the California Club and the Los Angeles Athletic Club.

> Los Angeles merchants were the civic and political leaders of their town. Without a class of leisured or professional men or even a clergy, and with the landholding patriarchs of Mexican days bankrupted, whatever there was of public or communal life was for merchants to organize. It was almost inevitable that the Jews, belonging almost entirely to this business group, appear prominently in civic affairs (Vorspan and Gartner, 1970).

More and more Jews came to Los Angeles in the early years, and a need developed for religious and communal facilities. In the mid-nineteenth century, a congregation, a cemetery, and a Hebrew Benevolent Society were established, and Jewish organizations became vehicles for Jewish education and mutual aid, as well as for the social activities of Jewish men and women. Even then most Jews were not observant, and some who were unmarried did not join the congregation or the Society, a separation from organized Jewish life that was a harbinger of later and more massive non-affiliation.

The first Jewish settlement was primarily in the downtown area with the community spreading out to create Jewish neighborhoods in East Los Angeles and South Central Los Angeles. Jews from Eastern Europe were attracted to the Boyle Heights area from older sections of the city and created two dozen synagogues and a number of important Jewish institutions that were the forerunners of others still serving the Los Angeles community. They established Congregation Talmud Torah in 1905 on Rose Street in downtown Los Angeles, but moved in 1912 to Boyle Heights where the Orthodox Congregation was called the Breed Street Shul. The Jewish Home for the Aged relocated to Boyle Heights in 1914, and in 1912 the Southern California Jewish Consumptive Relief Society was formed. It later became the Duarte Sanitarium and is now known as the City of Hope.

Boyle Heights was located east of the Los Angeles industrial district, and in the late 1920s and 1930s, the Jewish population grew to more than fifty thousand making it the largest Jewish neighborhood in the community. There were also large numbers of Mexicans there and smaller enclaves of Russians, Japanese, Armenian, and black populations. But ethnic succession has been a major factor of life in Los Angeles and, soon after World War II, most of the

Jews had left the area in moves to various parts of the metropolitan basin (Rochlin, 1984). Those who were more prosperous and acculturated moved to Wilshire, Hollywood, and West Adams, and later mobility took Jews to Beverly-Fairfax, Pico-Robertson, westward to the ocean, and to the San Fernando Valley.

In 1900 there were 2,500 Jews in Los Angeles who comprised a tiny fraction of the one million Jews living in the United States. By 1927 there were 65,000 including some who had first gained success elsewhere, others who resettled to escape such congested places as New York City and those who came for reasons of health. In spite of the restrictive immigration laws of 1924, another wave of immigration took place between 1936 and 1943 consisting of refugees from Hitlerism who tended to be of higher social and economic status. After World War II there was a further immigration of Jews who had survived Nazi atrocities, and who came to Los Angeles along with those energized by World War II and the post-war industrial-technological revolution.

About ten thousand Soviet Jews have come to Los Angeles since 1974 and, following the overthrow of the Shah in 1979, ten thousand Iranian Jews also came, creating the largest Iranian Jewish community in the country. There are many Israelis living in Los Angeles forming an almost invisible community, because they are dispersed and choose not to be visible (Sass, 1982). These migrations to Los Angeles, reinforced by the elderly and others seeking easier lifestyles, pushed the community to its present total of some half million Jews (see Table 1).

Those who moved to Los Angeles in the early days were often very different from each other coming from varied socioeconomic and cultural backgrounds, observing diverse customs and rituals, and praying from different texts. Ashkenazi Jews, those from Central Europe who were under German cultural influence, followed religious practices quite unlike those of the Sephardim, but there was considerable cooperation between them in the formation and maintenance of Jewish communal institutions. While the settlement in one place of so many Jews from various places sometimes led to misunderstandings, suspicion, and hostility, the pressures inherent in their common fate tended to stimulate the development of a full sense of community.

The Jewish experience in Los Angeles, indeed in America itself, was grounded in the values and principles unleashed by the French

TABLE 1

JEWISH AND CITY-COUNTY POPULATIONS IN LOS ANGELES*

Jewish Population		General Population		
			City	County
1850		1850	1,610	3,530
1860	100	1860	4,385	11,333
1870	20 families	1870	5,728	15,309
		1880	11,183	33,381
1881	136			
		1890	50,395	101,454
1900	2,500	1900	102,479	170,298
1904	3,000			
1907	7,000			
1910	5,795	1910	319,198	507,131
1912	10,000			
1917	20,000			
		1920	576,673	936,455
1923	43,000			
1927	65,000			
		1930	1,238,048	2,208,492
		1940	1,504,277	2,285,643
1941	130,000			
1946	168,000			
1948	260,000			
		1950	1,970,358	4,151,687
1951	315,000			
1959	391,000			
		1960	2,479,015	6,038,771
1970	444,934	1970	2,811,801	7,041,980
1980	503,000	1980	2,966,850	7,477,503
1983	501,000	1983	3,046,696	7,763,792
1984	500,870	1984	3,070,710	7,781,109

*Data compiled from U.S. Census Bureau, Vorspan and Gartner (1970), interview with Dr. Bruce A. Phillips (1985), L.A. City and County Planning Departments, and *American Jewish Yearbooks*.

Revolution and continued in the Enlightenment and the Emancipation. Secularization found a place in the religious and communal worlds of Judaism, and the espousal of universalist ideals, together with the rationalist philosophy of the late eighteenth and nineteenth centuries, contributed to the loosening of community bonds. A process was initiated in which Jews were freer to make choices about observing rituals, affiliation, or even declaring their Jewishness.

Jewish reformers in Europe and America sought to change the all-encompassing practices of traditional Judaism to make it another religion among the various religions and to help contemporary Jews function in the secular world. But the ancestors of most Los Angeles Jews came from countries in Eastern Europe that did not participate in the Emancipation, and for them the cultural shock was greater than for western Jews. Some came here right out of the ghettos and brought with them a Jewish language, lifestyle, and identity. This rich Jewish culture did not carry over fully into the next generation which desired to eliminate many vestiges of its immigrant history. A determination to become completely American led many to blend into the majority and to various ways of masking or denying their Jewish identity.

As Jews plunged into the secular society, Jewish communal agencies sought the full promise of the Emancipation through the removal of barriers to Jews in the general society along with the acquisition of equal rights and the elimination of prejudice and discrimination. At the same time, there were efforts to minimize Jewish distinctiveness and the impact of Jewish identity. The various institutions founded in Los Angeles around the turn of the century were geared to normalization and the blending of Jews with others in the general culture. Jewish religious life was Americanized and Jewish prophetic views were sometimes sacrificed in the quest for integration.

The weakening of traditional practices and commitment facilitated the separation from the synagogue of social, educational, and philanthropic activities as well as the creation of new Jewish institutions. Jewish fraternal orders like B'nai B'rith emulated the Protestant model of bourgeois communal involvement and, together with changes in religious practices brought about by the Reform movement, there was a further acculturation of Jews to Los Angeles. On the whole, Jews in the nineteenth and the early twentieth century lived a good life and their economic condition constantly improved. Synagogues in Los Angeles were well established, Jewish children attended public schools, and relationships with neighbors were friendly if not intimate.

The development of commercial banking and the railroads in the late nineteenth century ended the isolation of Los Angeles and led to the rapid growth of the Jewish and general populations. At the turn of the century, there was an influx of large numbers of Jews primarily from Eastern Europe. Many of the recent arrivals chose a religio-ethnic path different from that of the earlier German Jews, and Orthodox and Conservative synagogues were established for those who thought the pioneer Congregation B'nai B'rith (later the Wilshire Boulevard Temple) was not sufficiently traditional. Several more observant congregations were established in the 1890s and early 1900s consisting mostly of Russian and Polish Jews. The Moses Montefiore Hebrew Congregation was started in 1890 as a Conservative group whose more traditional perspective was a reaction to the practices of Reform Judaism. In 1902, Kahal Adath Beth Israel (the Olive Street Shul) was organized as an Orthodox congregation whose members were largely immigrants seeking to preserve the Judaism they remembered from Eastern Europe.

Most of the newcomers had not been permitted to be members of their national communities and they saw themselves as belonging to a separate people more than as products of a specific territory. They had and retained a Jewish ethnicity that was superimposed on a religious culture shaped by thousands of years of distinctive history. Their sense of ethnic self-consciousness and peoplehood encouraged the maintenance of religious Orthodoxy often through small communities of worshippers in rented halls. It also stimulated the development of Conservative Judaism as a movement that placed itself between the perceived asssimilationism of Reform Judaism and the communal isolation of Orthodox religion. By seeking acculturation in a new Jewish context that could harmonize tradition and change, Conservative Judaism appealed to many of the new immigrants who found Orthodoxy impractical and Reform unacceptable.

By the 1930s, fewer than half of Los Angeles' Jewish families belonged to any religious congregation, and even those who were religiously affiliated were often reflecting middle class behavior rather than genuine devotionalism or piety. Small Orthodox congregations were predominant in core areas of Los Angeles, but Conservative and Reform congregations were influential elsewhere.

More and more Jews moved to outlying areas, and the Reform movement that was so important in the early history of the community once again asserted itself as a major force in Los Angeles Judaism.

More than one hundred Jewish religious congregations are now to be found all over the Los Angeles area ranging from small to large, old to new, Reform to Orthodox. With the remarkable upsurge in traditional Judaism, Rabbi Maurice Lamm observed that Los Angeles had become "a fortress of centrist Orthodoxy" (*Present Tense,* 1982). Los Angeles was also impacted by a proliferation of Talmudic academies, such specialized Jewish institutions as synagogues for the performing arts and the deaf, as well as a gay Jewish congregation. Today, synagogue and rabbinic organizations serve the various branches of Judaism: the Union of American Hebrew Congregations (Reform), the United Synagogue of America (Conservative), and the Union of Orthodox Jewish Congregations. Other outlets of religious expression include the Sephardic congregations and the Hasidic and Reconstructionist movements; and the Southern California Board of Rabbis provides a forum for rabbinic discussion.

Jewish education was a matter of concern from the very beginnings of the Jewish experience in Los Angeles. Most Jewish students attended the public schools and Hebrew schools were first convened on weekday afternoons and later on Sundays. From the start, Jewish boys and girls participated in the study of Hebrew, biblical history, and religion. Other than in private lessons, however, there was very little formal study of the Talmud until after the turn of the century. The education of Jewish children was conducted essentially by the congregations, although a Yiddish Folk School was also established in the 1920s.

Orthodoxy contributed greatly to the establishment of day schools that offered an alternative to the growing number of Jewish supplementary schools. With the founding of a day school in 1935, the Los Angeles Jewish Academy, a serious attempt was made to strengthen the importance of Jewish education. This was followed in 1936 by the creation of the Bureau of Jewish Education which sought to encourage and enlarge the numbers of children educated and later to establish curricular and teaching standards for a meaningful Jewish education.

As Orthodoxy eroded among immigrants from Eastern Europe,

there was also a diminution of the Jewish folk tradition and the language, music, and literature that had evolved in centuries of ghetto and shtetl isolation. In order to strike a balance between Yiddish and American culture, the first Jewish Community Center was created in 1924 as a place where youngsters and adults could carry on various Jewish social and educational programs, hold their club meetings, and participate in recreational activities. Many of those who utilized the facilities of the centers were not especially rooted in religion or the synagogue, and the centers tended to serve as institutions in which the processes of acculturation to the American environment were stimulated and encouraged. From an early ideological stance grounded in humanistic concepts, the centers evolved as distinctive vehicles for Jewish education and identification. Today, a number of centers under the aegis of the Jewish Centers Association work to strengthen Jewish culture in settings that continue to be open to the non-Jewish community.

Jews from Eastern Europe were generally not welcomed with enthusiasm by the earlier acculturated residents who felt their tranquility was disturbed by those whose Yiddish-oriented culture contributed to the emergence of new hostilities. Those Jews who had been prominent in civic affairs began to suffer from virulent discrimination because of anti-Jewish stereotypes and hostility. The pattern of exclusion moved from social resorts, clubs, and civic groups to residential housing, employment, and education. There was discrimination in business, the professions, and universities, and quotas were adopted to limit the number of Jews who could participate in various endeavors. Hate groups emerged that proclaimed messages of Jewish inferiority, dishonesty, and racial conspiracy.

Anti-Semitism stimulated the creation of the Concordia Club that was later replaced by Hillcrest Country Club, Brentwood, and other largely Jewish social and recreational institutions. Jews were excluded from the California Club, the Chamber of Commerce, and other civic and communal groups they had helped to found. National Jewish "defense" organizations such as the American Jewish Committee, the American Jewish Congress, and the Anti-Defamation League of B'nai B'rith joined with the Jewish Community Relations Committee to combat rising bigotry and anti-Semitism, often in concert with minority, religious, and liberal groups. World War II linked anti-Semitism to the tragic course of events in Europe, and the response of Jewish organizations was to point out that American Jews had a vital stake in the fate of their relatives and coreligionists abroad and had to act on their behalf.

The strategies of the "defense" agencies sometimes varied as they utilized research, legal and legislative action, and programs of public education to eliminate prejudice and discrimination against Jews. In Los Angeles and elsewhere, Jews became very involved in the process of seeking a framework for Jewish life in the context of political and cultural freedom. This included the quest for full civil rights for all people, the strengthening of primary Jewish institutions, and the separation of church and state. All of the Jewish organizations were united in the belief that equality for Jews was tied to the availability of equal opportunity for all, a concept that led to the creation of the civil rights movement and its coalition of Jews, blacks, and other concerned groups. In recent years, however, the movement has been severely strained and coalitional strategies tend to focus on more specific areas of common interest.

Some Jews in the early part of the century became radicals and Socialists in the hope that the "Jewish question" would be solved through the universalistic message of justice and equality for all. Their secular ideology was accompanied by an opposition to Judaism and the substitution of humanism for religion. It was not a radicalism grounded in revolution, but rather a means of seeking and achieving a better life. As an educated, secularized urban people, others chose the liberal way of life as a substitute for the Jewishness of their parents. The American ideal was perceived as an extension of the Jewish tradition as Jews became leaders in the quest for a humane civilization in which ethnic and particularist commitments were to be eliminated.

Many Los Angeles Jews abandoned ritual and tradition under the impact of secularism, but they did not necessarily break with the ethnic or folk tradition that continued to prevail in the Jewish community. The concept of peoplehood proved to be an impetus for the Zionist movement among Jews who wanted to maintain their links to other Jews while coming to grips with the powerful forces of emerging world nationalism. As a movement, Zionism first appeared in Los Angeles at the turn of the century, becoming particularly vigorous in its varied ideological strains during the time of the European pogroms before World War I. Funds were raised to purchase land and to create institutions in Palestine, as well as to transport and settle a Jewish population seeking to reestablish a Jewish State. But the early promotion of Zionism that fostered a separate Jewish national-cultural entity with its own territory ran counter to the beliefs of those seeking to strengthen their rootedness in American culture.

The union movement enabled people who were powerless in Eastern Europe and America to join together more effectively in the power struggle with management. Factory working conditions for Jews and others were often very difficult and wages tended to be low. The problems faced by working men and women, especially in the needle trades, stimulated the development of trade unions to protect their interests. A local of the International Ladies Garment Workers Union was started in 1900 to organize Jewish tailors. Soon after, the Amalgamated Clothing Workers developed a collective bargaining process, and they were followed by bakers, millinery, cap, and fur workers also struggling for recognition. Labor turmoil and strikes ensued as the trade union movement in Los Angeles sought to advance the security and status of Jewish and non-Jewish workers.

The labor movement contributed materially to the acculturation of uprooted Jewish workers and helped them to settle into a strange new environment. Unions became vehicles for a struggle intended to refashion society and instill an ideological zeal based on the concepts of justice and righteousness inherent in Judaism. This process aided the upward mobility of Jews and made the Jewish labor movement essentially a one-generation phenomenon. The impulse toward reform and social change soon found its place in the Democratic Party where the Jewish political constituency was heavily concentrated.

Jews were also prepared for the American economic experience through a kind of Jewish puritanism that emphasized learning and study, foresight, moderation, and other habits leading to success in trade and the professions. Jewish "middle-class" values and the experience of Jews over the centuries as traders and businessmen helped them to achieve success in American middle-class pursuits. Those who migrated to Los Angeles came overwhelmingly from towns and villages, and their higher rates of literacy even in their native tongues marked them as different from the displaced peasants who characterized other European immigrant groups. Most had been involved in some kind of industry or commerce as compared to few of the other immigrants, and they included many skilled workers in different occupations and trades. Although they brought with them no stock or capital, they did possess as children or grandchildren of merchants and scholars a background in business and education as well as hard work. The process was similar to the earlier mass immigration of poor Jews from Germany, with many starting out as peddlers and small traders and, after a few years, becoming storekeepers and successful merchants.

Self-improvement through education was a fundamental tenet of the immigrant experience and contributed directly to the rapid upward mobility of Los Angeles Jews. The opportunity to get a formal education was extremely attractive and increasing numbers of Jews studied to become professionals in addition to those who sought business careers. Upward mobility began to stimulate the move to better neighborhoods as Jews learned to think of the ethnic neighborhood as a temporary stopping place, but this movement was accomplished largely in terms of a better standard of living and higher wages rather than social mobility and status which were generally denied to Jews.

By the 1930s, about one-half of the children came from homes where the fathers were workers, but one-third were now from homes where fathers owned businesses or were managers and officials. Later some Jews entered home building and commercial development, while others became stock brokers, corporate executives, and savings and loan entrepreneurs. As the economy of Los Angeles grew, a number of Jews were successful in family-owned retail and wholesale businesses and in such manufacturing enterprises as the garment industry.

Jews had their greatest visibility in the entertainment industry where they founded Columbia Pictures, Universal Studios, Warner Brothers, Paramount Pictures, and Metro-Goldwyn-Mayer. Many of the entertainers were also Jewish, but because of their fear of anti-Semitism, most changed their names. Today's Jewish entertainers do not hide their Jewish origins, and Jewish executives maintain a strong and visible presence in the film industry. Large numbers of Jews are also to be found in television, theater, and other areas of creative endeavor.

Years of prosperity have raised the ancestors of many East European Jews to the level of the earlier German Jewish residents. There are now few economic and occupational distinctions among

Jews of different national origins, and many of the younger generation are business and professional people who are better educated and wealthier than other segments of the population. There has been a significant increase in the number of Jews engaged in intellectual occupations and a decline among manual workers, white-collar workers, and salespeople. While many Jews are proprietors of their own businesses, their numbers have decreased and most Jews are now in salaried occupations.

Jews in Los Angeles and elsewhere were held together as a people aided by religious and communal institutions that evolved in changing political and cultural environments. New forms of Judaism and community structure developed that enabled Jewish life to survive in a kind of creative cultural synthesis. The rise of secular culture contributed to a shift from a religious and spiritual emphasis to an intellectual authority grounded in scientific rationality. Thus religious identification for many Jews came to involve more of a communal aspect than an expression of religious identity or commitment.

Although Jews were able to participate in many areas of Los Angeles life, much of their communal activity was carried on within a Jewish environment. Jews decided for themselves freely and voluntarily whether they wanted to associate with Jewish religious or communal endeavors. Voluntary associations proliferated throughout Los Angeles for purposes of mutual aid and assistance, and large numbers of Jewish organizations were founded including hospitals, fraternal groups, centers, and social clubs. Various institutions and facilities were created to care for the aged, orphans, and consumptives as well as to provide other health and social welfare services. The Federation of Jewish Charities was formed in 1911 in order to unify the various funding campaigns of some of these institutions. And landsmanschaften were organized for cultural activities and mutual aid among Hungarian, Rumanian, and Polish Jews.

In the early part of this century, there was a transition from charity assistance to a systematic approach to philanthropy and social welfare as fund raising through the Federation of Jewish Charities was gradually incorporated into the Community Chest. Federation became solely a planning and budgeting body, but a number of other Jewish institutions continued to raise funds directly. The *B'nai B'rith Messenger* (1914) reported "without fear of contradiction that the community has more charitable societies and institutions relatively, than any other city in the world."

But Jewish philanthropic needs could not be met by the Community Chest, especially in years of declining campaigns, and the United Jewish Welfare Fund (UJFWF) was organized in 1929 to raise funds for European Jewry and Palestine as well as local needs not supported by the Federation. Other organizational processes also developed for local welfare, community relations, and overseas relief, and in 1927 the Los Angeles Jewish Community Council was created with the UJFWF merged into the new body for centralized fund raising. In the late 1950s, the Jewish Community Council merged with the Federation of Jewish Welfare Organizations, and in 1959 they became the Jewish Federation Council of Greater Los Angeles.

Through effective funding campaigns and an increasingly centralized planning and budgeting process, considerable Jewish communal power emerged in the Federation Council as it was asked to underwrite the growth and development of Jewish schools, centers, youth activities, and a multitude of service programs. The movement toward local control of Jewish affairs was paralleled by a growing trend toward national centralization through such umbrella groups as the Council of Jewish Federations and the Presidents' Conference that harnesses support for Israel.

The Holocaust and the emergence of Israel tended to delimit ideological differences within the Los Angeles Jewish community while increasing a sense of communal cohesiveness. Fund raising and generating political support for Israel through groups like the American Israel Public Affairs Committee (AIPAC) have become the core elements of Jewish cultural and communal awareness. At the same time, a number of Jews working through such groups as the New Jewish Agenda have felt free to criticize particular actions taken by the government of Israel believing this did not diminish their support for the security of the State and the well-being of its people. For the most part, however, the Jews of Los Angeles limit their involvement in the internal affairs of Israel in the belief that the Arab threat to Israel's survival is a matter of more fundamental and primary concern.

Today, collective efforts are given expression through the vast array of organizations serving local, national, and overseas Jewish concerns. An institutional system has developed that serves a multiplicity of needs in such areas as support for Israel, Jewish education, and community relations along with more specialized requirements in the areas of health and social welfare. Individuals who lose their jobs and need employment guidance are assisted by the Jewish Vocational Service and those with personal problems receive counseling from the Jewish Family Service. Various mental health and psychiatric services are offered by Gateways Hospital, Hamburger Home, Julia Ann Singer Preschool Center, Vista Del Mar, and Reiss-Davis. Interest-free loans are available from the Jewish Free Loan Society and, over the years, a number of groups have been created to serve the disabled and senior adults. Cedars-Sinai Medical Center, dating back to the Kaspar Cohn Hospital of 1902, meets the health needs of many Los Angeles Jews. And in the spirit of general civic participation, its medical services are available to the entire community.

A large population of survivors moved to the Los Angeles area, and institutions and organizations were created to memorialize the Holocaust. The Federation now maintains a Martyrs Memorial and Museum of the Holocaust; the Simon Wiesenthal Center for Holocaust Studies carries out a broad array of educational programs; there is a UCLA Chair in Holocaust Studies; and fourteen survivors organizations develop educational programs. The children of survivors also organized to deal with the psychological problems that were to some extent passed on from the survivors, as well as to heighten awareness of what transpired during the Holocaust era.

Among the other significant Jewish groups established in Los Angeles are the Jewish Community Foundation, serving as an endowment fund to support innovative projects, and the Women's Conference which maintains close relations with Jewish women's groups like the National Council of Jewish Women, Hadassah, Pioneer Women, B'nai B'rith Women, and others. The Federation's Youth Department provides programs for Jewish youth throughout the community along with such other youth-serving institutions as the American Zionist Youth Foundation, Jewish Big Brothers, B'nai B'rith Youth, the National Conference of Synagogue Youth, the Southern California Federation of Temple Youth, United Synagogue Youth, and Jewish day and summer camps. Camp Ramah and Camp Hess Kramer serve as laboratories for living Judaism; Brandeis-Bardin Institute provides educational programs for Jews of all ages; and Hillel offers college students an opportunity to participate in cultural, religious, and communal activities.

Established in 1874, B'nai B'rith is the oldest continuing institution in the Jewish communal life of Los Angeles. As part of an international fraternal order, B'nai B'rith members combine humanitarianism and mutual aid as the guiding principles of their organization. From the early exclusivity of German-Jewish sponsorship, B'nai B'rith has evolved over the years as a large, essentially middle-class group that attracts many thousands of Jews to community service and Jewish self-awareness.

A Bet Din, a Jewish court founded in 1921, now functions to answer Halachic problems and to settle monetary, family, and personal disputes, and the more recent Bet Tzedek offers legal aid for the poor. Organized programs have become available for those who wish to convert, and there are synagogues that maintain a mikvah (ritual bath), Jewish mortuaries, cemeteries, and persons authorized to perform ritual circumcision. Jewish bookstores sell ritual objects, tefillin, mezuzot, yarmulkes, and other articles required for Jewish ceremonies, and one can find a number of strictly kosher restaurants, butcher shops, and bakeries (*Jewish Los Angeles*, 1982). And the Jerusalem-linked educational group Aish HaTorah works to provide Jewish nourishment among key leaders and young people.

Chabad-Lubavitch facilities throughout the community offer outreach programs for Jewish youth and others who require various helping services in a traditional, spiritual environment. Known for a mission of bringing secular or assimilated Jews back to its version of Judaism, Chabad has created a large number of communal service projects. They maintain drug rehabilitation centers, job training, a bookstore, ritual baths, and a synagogue for Russian immigrants. Although not fully accepted by the Jewish organizational establishment, their educational and social work programs have gained them substantial communal and financial support.

There are Jewish libraries, the prestigious Skirball Museum, and a Jewish Historical Society. Jewish writers, musicians, artists, and craftspeople specialize in such Judaica as folk dancing, Jewish cinema, theater, and choral groups. The Los Angeles Yiddish Culture Club and other groups continue their dedication to keeping the language alive; the Organization for Rehabilitation through Training sponsors vocational-technical schools; and the Jewish War Veterans and Jewish Labor Committee work to protect the rights of Jews. There are two national Yiddish newspapers that maintain

West Coast offices: *Jewish Daily Forward* and *Jewish Morning Freiheit*. Four local Jewish newspapers, the *B'nai B'rith Messenger, Heritage, Israel Today,* and the *Jewish Journal,* provide Jewish news of Los Angeles, the nation, and abroad. There are also Jewish magazines, radio and television programs, and student publications.

All of the elements for a fulfilling Jewish life are now present in this open and pioneering environment. A disparate but rather unified Jewish community has evolved on a voluntary basis with limited central authority. Individuals are free to join organizations or to ignore them, and large numbers of Jews in Los Angeles have chosen to become a part of organized Jewish life. With a majority of the Jewish population unaffiliated, however, the challenge for the future is the ability of the institutional Jewish community to reach out more effectively to the uninvolved so they also become a part of this rich and dynamic communual system.

II

Demography

Los Angeles has been greatly impacted by the mobility of Jews within America and throughout the world, with a significant number of Jews having come here from other places. The processes of adjustment to Jewish and communal life have been very complex and sometimes difficult as Jews also moved from place to place within the metropolitan area. Although Jews in Los Angeles are in better health and living longer than in the past, their numbers are no longer growing despite the continuing influx of new families. The projection is for later marriage or non-marriage, declining fertility and birth rates, more divorces, and an increase of intermarriage. Changing occupational patterns and a leveling off in the growth of socioeconomic status raise further questions about the condition of the Los Angeles Jewish community.

The Jewish population in Los Angeles is currently estimated at nearly 501,000 (see Table 1), but it is likely this figure does not include thousands of Jews who have overstayed their visas and avoid Jewish censuses. In its early experience, the Jewish community was a tiny minority, but it is now a major part of the Los Angeles scene representing the second largest concentration of Jews in the country. The first Jewish residents came largely from Germany and other Central European countries but, in the course of demographic changes, the current leadership of the organized Jewish community has developed primarily from those whose ancestors were from Eastern Europe.

Over the years, the residential patterns of Los Angeles Jews have changed appreciably as they moved from the largely Jewish central city and eastern areas to heavy concentrations on the west side, the San Fernando Valley, and the urban core in and around Fairfax. More recently, smaller settlements have developed in such outlying centers as the San Gabriel Valley and the southern region. The character of Jewish neighborhoods has been altered in the process with only 32.7% of Los Angeles Jews living in densely populated areas that are 45% or more Jewish, 46.5% in mixed areas ranging from 15% to 44% Jewish, and 20.8% in sparse areas less than 15% Jewish.

The location of the Jewish population is characterized primarily by the densely Jewish but racially changing urban core, the west side which runs from mixed to dense, and the San Fernando Valley whose spectrum moves from sparse to mixed to heavily Jewish. Younger Jews from ages 18 to 39 are more likely to be found on the west side, the 40 to 59 group in the Valley, and those 60 and over in the urban core. Among those who live in the urban core, the heaviest concentration is from the immigrant generation, while in the Valley and on the west side the third generation is predominant (see Table 2). The trend is toward living on the west side, followed closely by the Valley, but a return to the urban core is evident among some younger Jews.

The Fairfax area is the most Jewishly ethnic in Los Angeles with its Jewish food stores, restaurants, and religious and educational institutions. Over the years, the population has been reinforced by refugees from Nazi Germany, Orthodox and Hasidic Jews, new immigrants from Russia, and young families attracted to the lower housing costs and the area's Jewish qualities. There are many poor and working class Jews living there and, as the area undergoes the social, economic, and physical changes of urban life, new services are being provided for the elderly and others who need assistance. Efforts to revitalize Fairfax are supported by government and private institutions including Young Israel and the Jewish Federation.

Adjacent to this area is Pico-Robertson which has Orthodox, Conservative, and Hasidic congregations, kosher butcher shops, Jewish bookstores and day schools. Although it has always been a Jewish neighborhood, the influx of young Jewish families and Jewish businesses makes it a center of Jewish life that rivals the Fairfax district. Communally oriented Jews have also moved into the San Gabriel and Pomona Valleys and the South Bay area bringing with them a variety of organizations and institutions to serve local needs.

TABLE 2

GENERATIONAL DIFFERENCES WITHIN GEOGRAPHICAL AREAS

Generation	San Fernando Valley	Urban Core	West Side
First	19.3	35.5	15.3
Second	21.9	27.2	26.3
Third	40.4	28.0	40.2
Fourth	18.4	9.3	18.2
	100.0%	100.0%	100.0%

x^2, p. < .01

Jews on the west side live from Venice and Santa Monica to Westwood in an area that stretches from Beverly Hills to the ocean and from the top of the Santa Monica mountains to Culver City. A growing and visible Jewish community flourishes in a variety of neighborhoods with a number of Reform, Conservative, and Orthodox synagogues, Sephardic congregations, and one that is Reconstructionist. At the Bay Cities Synagogue in Venice, the Baal Teshuva (returnee) movement has given numerical strength and a great psychological lift to the Orthodox community. Many are young Jewish professionals who add another dimension to a population that is socioeconomically differentiated and culturally diverse.

The Jewish population of the San Fernando Valley includes over two hundred thousand Jews served by community centers, day schools, kosher butchers, and nearly thirty synagogues. Some of its early residents settled in Sun Valley which provided a healthier climate for asthmatics, but a widespread expansion of Jewish population developed explosively following World War II. Jews now live in all parts of the San Fernando Valley and have moved beyond to the Conejo-Simi and Santa Clarita Valleys. The two community-supported Jewish Homes for the Aging are located in Reseda along with a variety of other Jewish institutions (*Jewish Los Angeles*, 1982).

Los Angeles Jews tend to be stable occupants of neighborhoods with an average six years of residency as compared to three years for the general population. This stability has been reinforced in recent times by high interest rates for home loans and the enormous increase in property values, both of which limit opportunities for moving. Nonetheless, Jewish neighborhoods are changing as many no longer live next door to other Jews and lack the daily reinforcement of a Jewish environment.

Ethnicity is a paramount value that influences the patterns of association of individuals in a group, but most ethnics of the second, third, and subsequent generations are leaving their neighborhood enclaves and moving to heterogeneous suburbs where group identification is less relevant. Consequently, social class groupings are becoming cross-ethnic, particularly in the sprawling environment of Los Angeles. This geographical dispersion is highlighted by the belief that America permits and encourages upward mobility and that this may be very disruptive to the ethnic group. An increasingly affluent society tends to foster greater social and geographical mobility, thereby contributing to the decline of ethnic cohesion.

In the past, Jews lived near synagogues and Jewish helping organizations, benefitting from neighborhood networks and private intermediary institutions that provided social and psychological support. Today, many Los Angeles Jews live among and interact with a high proportion of non-Jews, and 84% report visiting a white Gentile home in the last three months. To meet the needs created by dispersal, a number of congregations, Jewish centers, and other institutions have been created in these new places of residence.

Interpersonal communication often depends on the automobile and the telephone which have become the indispensable links of a dispersed population. Mothers commute their children to Jewish schools; relatives and friends drive to social gatherings; and arrangements for various Jewish endeavors are made over the phone. New and less personal contacts are being developed through the use of the electronic media which offer Jewish content programs connecting Jews in various parts of the community. These processes have enabled Los Angeles Jews to maintain their Jewish identity through reference group associations and modern techniques of communication.

There is some contradiction in the attitudes and behavior of Los Angeles Jews in regard to their residential choices. While fewer than one-third live in a heavily Jewish area, more than half say that a Jewish neighborhood is a friendlier place to live. Those married to non-Jews as well as the unaffiliated are the most likely to live in a largely Gentile neighborhood, but many have dealt with the ambivalence in their lives by choosing to reside in mixed areas. Affiliated Jews tend to live in more densely Jewish places and are less likely to want to move, probably because they are satisfied with the Jewish character of their environments. It is particularly interesting that young, educated Jews, those under thirty, are the most desirous of having Jewish neighbors.

The data indicate that 93.4% of Los Angeles Jews express agreement with the statement: "I am glad I was born a Jew." This positive sentiment toward being Jewish is often acted out through the ways in which they maintain family relationships and select their closest friends. Of those who have relatives in Los Angeles, more than two-thirds see them very often and an additional 20% sometimes. The respondents reflect a range of friendship patterns, but almost three-fourths have Jews as their two closest friends. Those with the strongest Jewish identity are the most likely to have Jewish best friends, as are the affiliated, people who give generously to Jewish causes, and individuals who are fifty and over, especially with incomes of $40,000 a year or more. These patterns are undergirded by the fact that 58.8% of Los Angeles Jews say they feel more comfortable with other Jews.

The Los Angeles Jewish population tends to be considerably older than other subgroups in the area, with nearly half of the Jews fifty years of age or more. Respondents selected for the study were at least eighteen years of age and, of this group, the first and second generations are essentially over fifty and the third and fourth generations are largely under thirty. The percentage of Los Angeles Jews under thirty increases in a more or less straight line from the first to the fourth generations, while those fifty and over decline from the first to the third generations and level off in the fourth (see Table 3). Other demographic characteristics of the Los Angeles

Jewish community indicate that more than three-fourths were born in the United States, just over half are female, and nearly 20% served in this country's armed forces.

TABLE 3

AGE, BY GENERATION

Age	Generation			
	First	Second	Third	Fourth
18 - 29	10.4	11.5	43.7	55.8
30 - 49	14.3	20.6	42.9	30.2
50 and over	75.3	67.9	13.4	14.0
	100.0%	100.0%	100.0%	100.0%

x^2, p. $< .001$

Only 23% of Los Angeles Jews believe that having three or more children is "ideal" but, as the fertility rates of Jews decline, the fourth generation shows an increase in the desired number of children for a Jewish family (see Table 47). Orthodox Jews are also more likely than those who are less traditional to believe that having more children is important (see Table 14), as are those who are affiliated with a congregation. However, a negative assessment of the potential for increasing Jewish birth rates emerges in the analysis by socioeconomic status (SES). High SES Los Angeles Jews want fewer children, so that the likelihood of having more children declines with the upward mobility of Jews (see Table 4).

More than one-third of Los Angeles Jews are college graduates or higher, and those from ages thirty to forty-nine are the best educated. Jewish men are more likely than women to be college graduates, and better educated Jews tend to come from non-religious backgrounds, marry other college graduates who also had non-religious backgrounds, and are more likely to intermarry. Those

TABLE 4

IDEAL NUMBER OF CHILDREN FOR A JEWISH FAMILY, BY SOCIOECONOMIC SUBGROUPS

	Socioeconomic Status			
Ideal Number of Children for Jews	Low	Low-Low	High	High-High
0 – 2	35.3	53.7	65.4	62.7
3 – 6	64.7	46.3	34.6	37.3
	100.0%	100.0%	100.0%	100.0%

x^2, $p. < .05$

who are of Reform orientation are the most educated, followed by Conservative and then by Orthodox Jews (see Table 14).

Respondents were very cooperative in answering questions about family income, with 82.8% agreeing to do so. The data indicate that 31.6% have family incomes of under $15,000 a year, 35.4% range from $15,000 to $39,000, 21.9% are over $40,000, and 11.1% are students and retired persons who are often low income. The combination of families under $15,000 annual income with the high proportion of first and second generation retirees who tend to be lower income shows that nearly 40% of Los Angeles Jews are in an economically precarious position. This significant proportion of low income families is comparable to the data reported for Los Angeles Jewry in the *American Jewish Yearbook* (1985).

Low income status is generally believed to be a characteristic of elderly Jews but, in reality, significant segments of all generations are in the low income category. The third generation of Los Angeles Jews is the most affluent, but over 20% of this group have incomes below $15,000 a year. There is an increase of low income families in the fourth generation which suggests that some have not yet reached a peak of earning capacity or that the income of this generation is leveling off or even declining (see Table 5).

Economic networks among Los Angeles Jews are very comprehensive with a majority working for a Jewish or somewhat Jewish owner-management and strong social ties existing between Jewish co-workers. The data show that 37.2% are self-employed and that 27.2% are in a family-owned business. A trend away from ownership is apparent in the fact that only 13.3% expect family members to continue in the business after their retirement. In an analysis by generation, the percentage of family-owned businesses declines from the first to the second and third generations. However, there is a surprising upturn of ownership in the fourth generation which points up the possibility of a future trend toward entrepreneurship among Los Angeles Jews. This is reinforced by the relatively low desire of respondents to direct their children to professional occupations. Only 31.5% would like their sons to become professionals and 23.2% have this aspiration for their daughters. A greater proportion say they want their children to do what makes them happy or that it makes no difference which occupation they choose. It seems likely that the post-immigrant movement to the professions is slowing down, and that

Los Angeles Jews are moving toward new career directions and life satisfactions.

TABLE 5

ANNUAL FAMILY INCOME, BY GENERATION

	Generation			
Income	First	Second	Third	Fourth
Under $15,000	38.1	22.0	21.6	28.1
$15,000 to 39,000	14.3	29.6	38.1	31.3
$40,000 and Over	11.9	17.6	23.9	20.3
Retired, Students	16.7	13.2	2.2	4.7
Refuses	19.0	17.6	14.2	15.6
	100.0%	100.0%	100.0%	100.0%

x^2, p. < .001

Traditional concepts of marriage and child-rearing are undergoing enormous changes as the Los Angeles Jewish community is impacted by the new lifestyles of contemporary society. Among Los Angeles Jews eighteen years of age or older, more than half are married, one-fourth are single and never married, and almost 20% are divorced, widowed, or separated. The data indicate that 12.8% have been married two or more times, and that a higher proportion of men than women are married, with many more women than men divorced, widowed, and living alone. Individuals under thirty are the least likely to have married and those over sixty are the most likely to have married two or more times; the least educated tend to have the highest incidence of divorce. A Jewish Federation Council study underscores the problem by noting that the "normative" Jewish family is now a "minority" family in Los Angeles with only one out of four Jewish households including two adults and at least one child under eighteen (Phillips, 1980).

Patterns of Jewish mobility have had a greater impact on Reform Jews than on those who are Orthodox or Conservative (Waxman, 1981). Los Angeles Jews who are single are the most likely to have a Reform religious orientation, with the Orthodox the most married and Conservative Jews not far behind (see Table 6). Unaffiliated Jews are less likely to be married than the affiliated, with the decline in affiliation reinforcing the single status of Jews and threatening the traditional Jewish family.

TABLE 6

NUMBER OF TIMES MARRIED, BY RELIGIOUS ORIENTATION

	Religious Orientation		
Number of Times Married	Orthodox	Conservative	Reform
None	18.5	26.4	37.1
Once	65.8	62.4	51.5
Two or More	15.7	11.2	11.4
	100.0%	100.0%	100.0%

x^2, p. < .05

The growth of intermarriage among Los Angeles Jews is accompanied by an increase in the intergroup dating patterns of teenagers and adults, as well as by a greater tolerance toward more personal association with non-Jews. On the one hand, Jews tend to be clannish and to isolate themselves from intimate contact with Gentiles, and, on the other hand, their egalitarianism and belief in the ideals of an open, democratic society motivate them to be accepting of interpersonal relations with others.

The religious orientation of Los Angeles Jews is a factor in their attitudes and behavior toward interdating and intermarriage. Orthodox Jews are the most resistant to social interaction outside the Jewish group and Reform Jews are the least resistant (see Table 7). Nonetheless, such practices continue to grow in all subgroups, and the data show an increase of interdating across the generations (see Table 42). As socioeconomic status goes up, the limits placed by parents on the interdating of their sons and daughters declines (see Table 8), leading to a rise in the practice of interdating that is sometimes related to intermarriage.

The dating habits of Jewish adults are even less restrictive than teenagers as grown men and women are freer to make their own decisions. Adult interdating increases by generation, as well as among the less traditional and the unaffiliated (see Tables 42 and 7). It also goes up as socioeconomic status increases, until the fourth generation when interdating declines among Los Angeles Jews of the highest socioeconomic background. Jewish women are much more likely than men to always restrict their dating to other Jews, so that a significantly smaller percentage intermarry.

Individuals with a strong religious identity and sense of Jewish peoplehood are more likely to oppose the intermarriage of their children, but intermarriage continues to grow and most Jews are accepting of what is rapidly becoming the new condition of Jewish life. The data show that 17.0% of Los Angeles Jews have spouses who were born Christian, and an additional 3.2% have a different religious background or none. Among these families, few of the born Jews converted out of the Jewish religion, but about one-third of the non-Jewish spouses converted to Judaism. The percentage who have non-Jewish spouses increases in a straight line from the first to the fourth generations (see Table 42). There is also a differentiation by religious orientation with an intermarriage rate of 8.3% for the Orthodox, 20.0% among Conservative Jews, and 37.7% in the Reform group. Those who marry more than once tend to select a non-Jew in their subsequent marriages and, since divorce rates are increasing, this poses a further threat to the maintenance of Jewish family life.

Los Angeles Jews who are affiliated with a temple or synagogue are much more likely to have Jewish spouses, whether born into

TABLE 7

SOCIAL INTERACTION, BY RELIGIOUS ORIENTATION (%)

	Orthodox	Conservative	Reform	x^2, p. <
Always dated Jews as teenager	61.3	37.9	32.5	.001
Always dated Jews after teen years	49.3	25.9	15.1	.001
Had mostly Jewish friends as teenager	69.9	52.7	52.6	.01
Parents wanted respondent to stick with Jews in teen years	51.4	38.3	30.8	.01
Teen friends pressured respondent to avoid Gentiles	3.4	6.2	12.7	.01
Would restrict sons to dating Jews only	34.5	16.5	5.4	.001
Would restrict daughters to dating Jews only	34.9	20.7	7.9	.001
Would respond negatively to child's intermarriage	38.0	16.0	11.8	.001

TABLE 8

WOULD RESTRICT DATING OF SONS OR DAUGHTERS, BY SOCIOECONOMIC STATUS (%)

	Socioeconomic Status (SES)				
Would Restrict Dating	Low-Low	Low	High	High-High	x^2, p. <
of son	40.0	23.5	17.1	6.8	.01
of daughter	43.8	27.3	19.6	10.4	.01

Judaism or converted (see Table 9). The rate of intermarriage is much higher among unaffiliated Jews of all generations, rising to an extraordinary 66.7% among the unaffiliated of the fourth generation. While there is also an increase of intermarriage among affiliated Jews, the rate of growth is much lower and tends to level off between the third and fourth generations.

TABLE 9

AFFILIATED WITH A CONGREGATION, BY RELIGION OF SPOUSE

	Religion of Spouse	
Affiliated	Jewish	Other
Yes	37.1	9.8
No	62.9	90.2
	100.0%	100.0%

x^2, p. $<$ .01

The respondents were asked if any of their children had married non-Jews and 25.9% responded affirmatively. Intermarriage of children is highest among parents who have had the least Jewish education and, when examined by socioeconomic status, those at the very lowest and very highest ends of the scale show the lowest rates of intermarriage for their children. The data indicate that the highest rate of intermarriage is among the children of working and middle-class Jews, and the lowest is among those with the highest socioeconomic status (see Table 10). This suggests that for these in the highest SES group, their permissiveness toward interdating (see Table 8) is not yet reflected in the behavior of their children.

In regard to the responses of parents if their children were to marry non-Jews, there is relatively little opposition or resistance. Men, young people under thirty, those who are the least educated

TABLE 10

HAVE INTERMARRIED CHILDREN, BY JEWISH EDUCATION AND SOCIOECONOMIC STATUS (%)

	Jewish Education Index			
	Little or None	Moderate	Strong	x^2, p. <
Have any children married non-Jews?	33.7	18.1	18.2	.05

	Socioeconomic Status				
	Low-Low	Low	High	High-High	
Have any children married non-Jews?	16.7	39.2	21.8	11.8	.01

Jewishly or otherwise, and persons who themselves married non-Jews tend to be the least opposed. Affiliated Jews are more resistant, but this group also tends to show considerable acceptance of the possibility of intermarriage. Nearly half of the unaffiliated and one-fourth of the affiliated even say they would be happy if a child married a non-Jew (see Table 11).

The religious backgrounds into which their spouses were born frequently impact on the attitudes and behavior of Los Angeles Jews. This is particularly true of intermarrieds who are far less likely to want a bar or bat mitzvah for their children, to send them to Jewish summer camps, to encourage them to stick primarily with other Jews, or to oppose their interdating or intermarriage. In light of the very high and growing proportion of Jews marrying out of the group, the potential for permanent losses to the Jewish community is increasing. These data raise questions about the hypothesis of Silberman (1985) that Jewish continuity is not endangered by intermarriage.

The problem is reinforced by upward movement in the occupational and social systems which is stimulated by secular education, geographic mobility, and the opportunities afforded by an open democratic society. As discrimination has diminished, Jews have been accepted increasingly in the professions and major business enterprises that have required them to relocate. This has been accompanied by a rise in rootlessness and alienation as many have left the protective environments of the home, the friendship group, and the supportive neighborhood. Among the major consequences of this disruption has been a change in the patterns of Jewish family life and communal participation.

To cope with changing conditions in society, new programmatic approaches are being developed that are intended to encourage the transmission of Jewish values in activities that provide both realistic support for the family and meaningful Jewish content. The family continues to be the basic support group for most people, but help can also come from friends, neighbors, and religious and communal institutions. Many organizations are now offering day care for single parents and working-class families and counseling for lonely singles, divorced parents, and alienated youth. Neighbors watch the unattended houses of friends, take care of their children, and assist in illnesses. And temples and synagogues frequently offer a kind of extended family underpin-

TABLE 11

AFFILIATION (INDEX), BY RESPONSES TO POSSIBLE INTERMARRIAGE OF A CHILD

	Disown, Insist on Conversion	Not like, but Accept	Not care, Accept, No Opinion	Be Happy	Total
Unaffiliated	2.3	13.0	36.7	48.0	100.0%
Affiliated	8.0	23.9	44.8	23.3	100.0%

x^2, $p. < .001$

ning that can provide social and psychological assistance in times of personal need.

What is often lacking, however, is an intensification of efforts to reach out to individuals and families who are not connected with Jewish communal life. This is particularly important because many Jewish institutions are still largely geared toward the traditional family and lack the capacity to adjust to the growing tension between individualistic goals and family and group needs. At the core of much of the difficulty is the fact that large numbers of Jews in dire economic straits do not have the ability to pay for the religious, educational, and social services they require.

When the very critical demographic changes affecting Jewish family and community life are assessed, including the processes of intermarriage, the emergence of alternate lifestyles, a decline in marriages, reduced rates of fertility, the growth of divorces, and increasing patterns of mobility, it seems evident that new and creative means are essential to stem the flow of Jewish communal losses. A systematic program of outreach is needed to facilitate the involvement of the unaffiliated in Jewish communal processes, for without needed adjustments by the institutions and leadership of the organized Jewish community, concern must be expressed for the long-term future of Jewish life in Los Angeles.

Section 2

Jewish Identity

Introduction to Section 2

Religion used to be the key defining characteristic of a multifaceted Jewish identity. This has been overlaid, but not completely replaced, by ethnic Jewishness—a sense of peoplehood or national identity. In secular, pluralist western societies where membership in the Jewish community is a matter of free choice, Jewish ethnic and cultural behaviors have become characteristic (American Jewish Committee, 1972). Individual Jews are less Jewish in some ways, but they are more closely tied in others. They give more to Jewish causes, are more united in communal activities, and are more openly active in terms of their own interests. American Jewry has been able to fashion both a Jewish and American identity that affirms Jewish peoplehood in this country, Israel, and throughout the world.

The Nazi crusade that led to the Holocaust intensified the sense of uniqueness felt by Jews as well as the universal quality of Jewish identity. A consequent increase in anti-Semitism brought Jews together across denominational lines while activating non-religious Jews who might otherwise have left the community. Jewish identity was also aroused by threats to the safety of Israel, and the ensuing support for Israel represented a secular and ethnic outlet for Jewish expression that was not necessarily religious. In this process, a generation of Jewish leaders became involved in a vast rescue and rehabilitation effort that generated feelings of identification and unity with Jews throughout the world.

It is clear that Jewish identification in contemporary America is quite heterogeneous in terms of religious and personal practices, as well as socioeconomic and political status. To help measure the varieties and the salience of Jewish identity, a group cohesiveness scale was constructed that was based on earlier research (Sandberg, 1974). A review of the literature and consultation with a widely representative panel of experts from Jewish religious, educational, and social science backgrounds, produced a broad-gauged psychological measure of Jewish identity. The model employs the classic formulation of Jewish religious, cultural, and national (peoplehood) variables (Kaplan, 1934) that, interrelated, constitute a measure of Jewish identity and facilitate the analysis of differential degrees of Jewish identification (see Table 30 and Appendix).

The study of Jewish religious identity necessitated the creation of a religious identity construct with subscales measuring the devotional and communal elements of Judaism (Lenski, 1963). The devotional subscale includes a number of attitudinal items concerning personal feelings about prayer and synagogue participation. The communal subscale uses items measuring the respondent's feelings about the value of the synagogue for those in the kinship group as well as personal responsibility for reaching out to others. The devotional and communal aspects reinforce each other and can also be seen as part of a total measure of religiosity.

Jewish cultural identity is assessed through various indicators in the cultural subconstruct of the Jewish identity scale. A number of elements are utilized apart from national and religious identity to help differentiate the reactions of individuals to the meaning of Jewish culture. The respondents were asked to respond to the importance of Jewish cultural groups, media, history, tradition, literature, music, language, and education, as well as their willingness to support the preservation of the Jewish cultural heritage.

In order to assess the importance to individual Jews of group cohesiveness and loyalty, the national (peoplehood) subconstruct of the Jewish identity scale presented a number of items for psychosocial responses. These include questions on ethnic solidarity and the extent to which social intercourse with other groups has been inhibited. Scale items help to examine feelings pertaining to Israel, kinship, ingroup responsibility, and the desire to associate with others of similar backgrounds. The national (peoplehood) subscale distinguishes between religious and cultural factors in the assessment of Jewish identity and is a special component in this analysis.

Most Americans identify themselves with some kind of subgroup whether it is Jewish, European ethnic, or regional, but the marks of identification are sometimes symbols without much social content or distinction. Jews participate in their rites of passage which are ceremonial and of great importance, but which do not take a lot of time or interfere with their regular lives. This kind of symbolic ethnicity is usually practiced through the rites of circumcision, bar and bat mitzvah, high holy day observances, or possessing a menorah, mezuzah, or Bible. Jewish ethnicity is also symbolized by the purchase of Jewish foods, magazines, and books, going to Jewish vacation resorts, and other ingroup recreational and social activities. The political way of expressing symbolic ethnicity finds Jews sending large amounts of money to Israel and using political pressure in support of their perceived interests (Gans, 1979).

Ethnicity is seen by some as a counter-rational, uncontrollable social force that leads to hatred and violence and is the enemy of enlightenment and liberalism. However, this confuses nationalism or tribalism with cultural heritage and is not particularly sensitive to the varieties of people in our society (Novak, 1977). In reality, ethnicity is emerging as a new social category, as significant as that of social class. The liberal expectation that distinguishing group characteristics were to lose their meaning in modern society, and the radical expectancy that class would become the main line of division, eliminating tribalism, are being challenged by the ways in which ethnic groups are behaving as interest groups. Ethnic-based forms of social identification and conflict are emerging in which the emphasis has shifted from culture, language, and religion to the economic and social interests of the group (Glazer and Moynihan, 1974).

While individuals are aligned with members of a particular group, they are also marked off or mark themselves off from members of other groups (Herman, 1977). This is reinforced by the hierarchy of statuses in American culture in which some groups are valued more than others. Belonging to a socially stigmatized minority group carries with it major psychological implications (Goffman, 1963), for when human beings are relegated to an inferior status they doubt themselves and question their value and worth, as well as that of the group to which they belong (Lewin, 1948). Personality problems can arise among Jews seeking to maintain their Jewish identification, with a consequent increase in sensitivity about their Jewishness.

But Jewish identity is more than merely a response to Gentile dislike. Those who identify positively with their Jewishness have high self-esteem, low self-denigration, and are able to synthesize positive and negative associations with the group in order to form an attachment to it. The process of creating an identity out of various identifications is very complicated as Jews try to resolve the conflicting social forces within their own psyche. An early, clear, and positive feeling of belonging to the group can be an essential foundation to the individual's security, direction, and identity (Klein, 1980).

The formation of identity involves an interactive process between the core elements of personality and the social forces encountered in the culture, producing a unique product for each individual, although many of its components are socially shared (Kelman, 1980). The realization of identity continues throughout the life cycle starting in childhood and relating to family, peer, sexual, socioeconomic, religious, cultural, and national identifications. Identity is developed in largely unconscious ways through the internalization of a series of identifications so that identity emerges as a "new combination of old and new identification fragments" (Erikson, 1968). All significant identifications are altered in the process of identity formation to make them part of a unique, coherent whole (Erikson, 1960). Jewish identity, therefore, reflects the various identifications and behaviors acquired by Jews in their involvements with human culture and experience.

The Jewish family has been the basic instrument of Jewish socialization and identity formation, and family practices that reflect Jewishness are adopted by the child along with others that become ritualized behaviors. Exposure to Jewish experiences and folkways varies from community to community and family to family. Those less intensively exposed are often left with a weaker identity core than those more intensively exposed. When family life is interwoven with ethnic practices, the child has the psychological benefit of meaningful rituals and ceremonies such as religious observances, holidays, family events, and rites of passage (Sebald, 1968).

Adolescents are eager to be affirmed by their peers and ready to be confirmed by rituals, creeds, and programs related to those social values that influence their identity formation and help them to succeed in the adult world. Since ethnic and moral systems are fixed in late adolescence and early adulthood, exposure to Jewish traditions at this time facilitates their incorporation into the ego ideal system. This comes not only from the imitation of parents and contemporaries, but through Jewish education, teacher influence, and other intellectual and social inputs.

During adolescence a young person may also seek to reject the influence of parents as well as aspects of an earlier identification with them. This may not be a permanent phenomenon but, rather, a temporary inactivating that retains a potential to reemerge if the need arises in the future (Ostow, 1977). Those who do not successfully go through the process of ego synthesis during this period are likely to be subject to identity diffusion.

Most Jews are not deeply involved in organized Jewish community life, but continue to identify themselves as Jews while remaining unaffiliated. They maintain loyalty to a tradition and commit their children to it while they themselves are not religiously or even communally involved. There is among many a longing for community that is not satisfied by current Jewish institutional forms, and numerous Jews feel they are outsiders. Some Jews cannot afford to participate and others are stigmatized because they are unmarried, divorced, unsuccessful, or because they are converts or children of a converted mother (Motz, 1977-78).

Still, Jewish organizations persist and thrive as places where opportunities are provided for associational involvements that reinforce ties among community members. The emphasis today is not on the discipline of religious behavior, but on the discipline of organizational obligation and responsibility. Many feel that serving the established community, especially particular organizations, is a means of expressing Judaism in their lives, a uniquely American version of a secular and moralistic Jewish identification. Organizational programs constitute the ideologies of the community, and organizational culture becomes the embodiment of Jewish identity (Weisberg, 1964).

Nearly half of the adult Jewish population in this country report membership in a synagogue, many others belong to Jewish organizations, and there is a significant degree of overlap (Massarik and Chenkin, 1973). But there is a particular problem in large communities because the percentage of those affiliated with Jewish religious and communal institutions tends to decrease as the size of the community increases. The combined rates of religious and communal affiliation in such communities as Nashville, Dallas, Providence, and Lakeville is approximately 90%, while in larger cities it is far lower (American Jewish Committee, 1980 and Sklare and Greenblum, 1967). Lower rates of affiliation are reported in communities such as Atlanta where there have been recent population gains (Metropolitan Atlanta Jewish Population Study, 1985). Jewish women are more likely to be affiliated with Jewish groups than are men (Goldstein and Goldscheider, 1968), but women continue to represent a largely untapped resource in Jewish life.

Recent Gallup Polls show that religious attendance is declining with 40% of the adult population regularly attending services and only 20% of Jews attending regularly (*New York Times,* December 30, 1979). While many Jews continue their attachment to the synagogue, this is often more cultural than specifically religious. For them, synagogues have become social forums, benevolent societies, and centers for various Jewish activities including recreational and educational programs, lectures, art classes, and golden age clubs. Consequently, the ties binding Jews to their religion are weaker than those of Protestants or Catholics, while the ties binding them to one another are much stronger (Lenski, 1963). A Connecticut Mutual Life report (1981) indicates that the level of religious commitment of Jews is the lowest of the major faith groups in America. The study shows 33% of Protestants highly involved in religion, compared with 15% of Catholics and only 3% of Jews.

At the same time, there is among some Orthodox, Conservative, and Reform Jews a renewed interest in Judaism as well as in Halacha (Jewish law). A number of Jews see Halacha as a means of expressing themselves ethnically while others see it more as a traditional religious phenomenon (Dorff, 1981). There is also a new kind of religiosity in this country stemming from disillusion with materialism and hedonism, and some young adults both affiliated and unaffiliated, are stimulated to various forms of Jewish revival and involvement. While traditional practices have declined, there is an increased emphasis on high holiday and seder participation, fasting on Yom Kippur, and the more American-oriented Chanukah candlelighting.

For religiously affiliated Jews, the synagogue has become an all-embracing institution that provides a framework for religious observance and prayer as well as social and political activities. It is a service center for celebration of the rites of passage, a place for Jewish education and recreation, as well as a vehicle for promoting Jewish identity and survival. For them, the synagogue functions as a subcommunity for the Jewish extended family and facilitates the processes of religious, social, and psychological support so essential to the strengthening of Jewish life.

III

Religious Identity and Affiliation

Throughout the history of the Los Angeles Jewish community, there has been substantial participation in Jewish religious and organizational life. More recently, however, great concern has developed about the diminishing rates of affiliation among Los Angeles Jews. Membership in Jewish institutions is generally considered a key indicator for measuring how Jews identify themselves and, as Jews have moved away from their neighborhoods and traditional centers of Jewish involvement, the decline in affiliation has been evidenced in both synagogues and Jewish communal institutions.

Estrangement from traditional Jewish institutions, together with indifference and a generally low level of Jewish education, constitute a real threat to the survival of the Jewish community in Los Angeles. The unprecedented freedom that Jews enjoy, the size and mix of the Los Angeles population, and a reduction in peer pressure all contribute to the drifting away from Jewish structures. Jewish family and friendship networks, various forms of symbolic Jewish identification, and a concern with Jewish issues have, in a sense, become surrogates for organizational ties and involvement. But the move away from Jewish institutions to informal expressions of Jewishness may not be enough to transmit the meaning and vitality of Jewish life to future generations.

Those who are formally identified with the non-congregational Jewish community see their organizations as doing good work in assuring the safety and survival of Jews in Israel and throughout the world while, at the same time, strengthening the educational, social welfare, and security needs of Jews in Los Angeles and across the country. Membership in Jewish organizations also helps to mediate the crisis in Jewish identity experienced by some of those who cannot commit themselves fully to the Jewish religion.

Jewish religious life in Los Angeles is marked by a declining rate of affiliation, limited participation, and diverse ways of religious expression and identification. There tends to be an inverse ratio between the size of a community and the rate of Jewish religious affiliation. In smaller communities, most Jews belong to congregations because that is the norm of religio-communal behavior, but in large cities like Los Angeles there is a much lower rate of affiliation.

Still, there are many temples and synagogues in the metropolitan area representing a wide range of denominational and institutional ideologies and forms. Storefront shuln are interspersed among cathedral-like Reform and Conservative temples, and even the Orthodox have built imposing physical structures. As the Jews of Los Angeles move increasingly out of Jewish neighborhoods into mixed or Gentile areas, synagogues and their institutional systems help to provide needed social and psychological support.

An affiliation index was constructed in order to measure formal identification with the organized Jewish community, with those who belong to a temple or synagogue, to a Jewish communal organization, or to both considered affiliated. The very low rates of affiliation in Los Angeles are reflected in the data that show 28.9% belonging to one or more religious congregations and 27.2% belonging to one or more Jewish communal organizations. The data further indicate that 44.9% are members of either or both, while 55.1% are organizationally unaffiliated (see Table 12). Another way of looking at these relationships is that they are mutually reinforcing, with more than 40% of those who belong to a Jewish organization also belonging to a synagogue.

The decline in religious affiliation is shown by the fact that 45.3% of the respondents were members of congregations at some time, with the figure dropping to 27% in 1968 (Massarik, 1968) and leveling off to the present. There has also been a considerable generational decline in the rate of affiliation with Jewish communal organizations from the 53.8% membership rate reported for their parents to the present level of 27.2% among respondents.

Affiliated and unaffiliated Jews in Los Angeles can be distinguished in a variety of ways in terms of their Jewish attitudes and behaviors. The affiliated tend to express themselves consistently in a manner that displays their Jewish commitment, but the unaffiliated also reflect a considerable awareness of and concern with Jewish interests. In some areas such as the security of Israel and combatting anti-Semitism, the affiliated and unaffiliated are fairly similar in their outlooks. Nonetheless, the affiliated are far more likely to have a stronger Jewish identity, to give to Jewish causes, to have been to Israel or plan to go there, to send their children to Jewish schools and camps, to live in a Jewish neighborhood, and to object to the interdating or intermarriage of their children. They are also inclined to be more observant, to have had more Jewish friends as teenagers, to be married, and to have had a Jewish first spouse.

TABLE 12

BELONG TO JEWISH RELIGIOUS OR COMMUNAL INSTITUTIONS OR BOTH (%)

Belong to one or More Jewish Congregations	Belong to One or More Other Jewish Organizations		
	No	Yes	Total
Yes	17.7	11.2	28.9
No	55.1	16.0	71.1
Total	72.8	27.2	100.0%

Los Angeles Jews affiliated with a congregation tend to have high levels of interest in and satisfaction with their temples and synagogues, with more than 70% feeling it is important to contribute their time and resources to the congregation. They also like to be with other Jews at religious services and enjoy participation in synagogue programs. It is primarily in the area of religious devotion or piety that a shift in belief occurs, with 86.7% acknowledging the Jewish faith is a source of real strength but only 55.3% feeling prayer helps them when troubled. This suggests that many Jews are affiliated with congregations to satisfy communal rather than spiritual needs. The value of prayer has declined consistently over the generations among the unaffiliated, but an upsurge of belief is evident among fourth generation affiliated Jews. With respect to fourth generation, high socioeconomic status affiliated Jews, 58.9% express the view that prayer helps them when they are troubled.

Some Los Angeles Jews with a weak religious identity belong to synagogues and, conversely, a substantial proportion of those with a strong religious identity are unaffiliated. The data indicate that 12.5% of those with a low religious identity are members of a congregation, but 54.6% of Los Angeles Jews who rate high on the religious identity scale do not belong. Since a high proportion of Jews with a strong religious identity are unaffiliated, there appears to be a large reservoir for potential involvement in organized religious life (see Table 13).

TABLE 13

AFFILIATED WITH A CONGREGATION, BY JEWISH RELIGIOUS IDENTITY

	Religious Identity	
Belong to a Congregation	Low	High
Yes	12.5	45.4
No	87.5	54.6
	100.0%	100.0%

x^2, p. < .001

Among Los Angeles Jews who claim membership in a temple or synagogue, 18% are Orthodox, 47% Conservative, and 33% Reform. These figures are slightly higher for Orthodox and Conservative Jews and a little lower for Reform Jews than those of the study conducted in 1980 by Bruce Phillips for the Jewish Federation Council of Greater Los Angeles. Dr. Phillips shows the affiliated as 15% Orthodox, 43% Conservative, and 37% Reform. The differences may be explained by the fact that the Federation study includes a larger sample of Jews in outlying areas who tend to be less traditional. Both data sets are similar to those of the National Jewish Population Survey of 1971 (Massarik and Chenkin, 1973) which indicates the affiliated as 14% Orthodox, 49% Conservative, and 34% Reform.

The respondents were asked about their religious orientation, and one-fourth classified themselves as secular, atheist, or agnostic. Among those with a particular religious orientation, there are clear and consistent patterns that underscore the strongest traditional attitudes and behavior among the Orthodox, followed by Conservative, and then Reform Jews. Table 14 points up the high proportion of Orthodox and Conservative Jews and the lower proportion of Reform Jews who have had any formal Jewish education. However, the Orthodox of Los Angeles clearly have a greater knowledge of Hebrew than either of the others.

Those of Orthodox orientation are the most likely to have come from a Jewish religious background and to have married someone of similar background, followed by Conservative, and then Reform Jews. Orthodox Jews are also the most likely to plan to send children to afternoon or all-day schools, to believe that Jews should have larger families, and to want their sons to have a bar mitzvah, although fewer Jews of all denominations want a bat mitzvah than a bar mitzvah. With respect to the Jewish education of their children, Conservative and Orthodox Jews have the strongest interest in Sunday schools and in Jewish summer camps. Those of various denominational orientations have a similar desire to send their children to programs in Israel with the small differences not statistically significant (see Table 14).

Los Angeles Jews who belong to a congregation are more likely to have had a strong Jewish education than those who belong only to a Jewish communal group. Still, a considerable number of the Jewishly educated are not affiliated with either a congregation or a

TABLE 14

CULTURAL CHARACTERISTICS, BY RELIGIOUS ORIENTATION (%)

	Orthodox	Conservative	Reform	x^2, p. <
Had formal Jewish education	80.8	78.1	63.2	.01
Understands Hebrew	51.0	34.9	34.3	.01
College graduate or higher	31.9	42.5	50.4	.01
Born into Jewish religious background	92.7	61.8	44.2	.001
Spouse born into Jewish religious background	77.1	56.3	46.4	.001
Sons should have bar mitzvah	91.8	74.4	38.1	.001
Plans to send child to afternoon school	75.0	58.3	27.7	.001
Plans to send child to parochial school	14.3	6.6	5.5	.05
Ideal number of children for Jewish couple is three or more	54.4	39.5	36.6	.01
Plans to send child to Sunday school	63.0	74.8	32.6	.001
Plans to send child to Jewish summer camp	56.7	52.3	32.2	.01
Plans to send child to programs in Israel	26.7	28.4	21.6	n.s.

Jewish communal organization. Across the generations, the percentage of those who have received a moderate or no Jewish education has increased among both the affiliated and unaffiliated. The data show that 61.1% of the fourth generation unaffiliated have had little or no Jewish education and only 7.4% of the fourth generation affiliated report a heavy Jewish education. Moreover, 36.3% of Los Angeles Jews who belong to a congregation have had little or no Jewish education.

There are continuing signs of interest in Jewish subjects manifested in both the informal reading habits and more formal adult education courses taken by Los Angeles Jews. Although unaffiliated Jews show some interest, the affiliated are much more likely to have taken Jewish college or adult education courses or to be currently reading books on Jewish topics, Jewish newspapers, and magazines. The desire to pursue Jewish intellectual interests continues across generations, with a noticeable increase among fourth generation affiliated Jews of high socioeconomic status.

Those who are religiously affiliated are very selective about traditional forms of observance and have developed a new consensus of what is deemed to be acceptable religious behavior. Rituals and holidays that require the least ongoing obligation or sacrifice are the most kept, including attendance at high holiday services and Passover seders, fasting on Yom Kippur, and lighting Chanukah candles. Religious requirements calling for frequent and regular observance are performed less often, including lighting Sabbath candles, buying kosher meat, and keeping separate dishes. The unaffiliated also reflect selective patterns of observance, with considerable interest shown in attending seders and high holiday services, fasting on Yom Kippur, and lighting Chanukah candles (see Table 15). As for regular attendance at Sabbath services, the affiliated are obviously far more likely to attend than the unaffiliated. In the first generation, more than one-third of the affiliated attend regularly, but this declines to approximately one-fourth among the affiliated of the second, third, and fourth generations.

About half of the Jews in Los Angeles report regular attendance at high holiday services, with the first and second generations attending more frequently than the third or fourth generations. Attendance at high holiday services among the affiliated increases from the third to the fourth generations, but it declines from the second to the fourth generations among the unaffiliated. In using the affili-

TABLE 15

RELIGIOUS AFFILIATION, BY OBSERVANT BEHAVIOR (%)

Belongs to Temple or Synagogue	Always, Usually Observe						
	Lights Sabbath Candles	Attends Seders	Buys Kosher Meat	Lights Chanukah Candles	Keeps Separate Dishes	Attends High Holiday Services	Fasts on Yom Kippur
Yes	40.3	89.9	27.7	86.6	18.5	89.9	74.3
No	8.9	58.4	5.8	46.0	2.1	31.1	37.0

x^2, $p. < .001$

ation index that includes Los Angeles Jews who are members of religious and, or, communal groups, attendance among fourth generation affiliated Jews is the highest and among fourth generation unaffiliated Jews the lowest of any of the generational subgroups (see Table 16). When the data are controlled further by socioeconomic status (SES), both high and low SES, affiliated fourth generation Jews continue to manifest strong patterns of attendance.

More than two-thirds of Los Angeles Jews report always or usually attending a seder, with participation substantially greater than for high holiday services among both affiliated and unaffiliated Jews in Los Angeles. The cost of congregational memberships or the purchase of tickets for services is a deterrent for some who find no such barriers to joining in seders. The high level of seder involvement among the unaffiliated suggests that seders may be more an ethnic than a religious phenomenon with the gathering of family and friends also a motivating factor. Seder attendance stays consistently high across the generations for the affiliated, but there is a decline from the second to the fourth generations among unaffiliated Jews (see Table 17). When controlled for generation and socioeconomic status, the continuing generational decline is especially apparent among high SES unaffiliated respondents.

Fasting on Yom Kippur is gaining favor among fourth generation Jews affiliated with a congregation after the practice declined considerably in the third generation, thereby underscoring the fourth generation "return" of affiliated Jews. Although the practice has been reduced among the unaffiliated, many of those in the fourth generation also continue to fast on Yom Kippur. Lighting Sabbath candles has declined steadily among the unaffiliated until it is almost nonexistent, but the drop among affiliated Jews has leveled off with more than one-quarter of the fourth generation maintaining this ritual. The various data indicate that, in general, religious practices have declined from the first to the third generations, with a fourth generation return in certain practices among affiliated Jews.

People tend to identify themselves symbolically through a variety of "passive" behaviors that require little or no effort or time. Among Los Angeles Jews, 72.6% report owning a prayer book or Bible, 66.3% have a menorah, and 44.1% have a kiddush cup. Affiliated Jews are more likely to possess these objects but, depending on the item, from one-third to one-half of the unaffiliated also have them.

TABLE 16

HIGH HOLIDAY ATTENDANCE OF AFFILIATED AND UNAFFILIATED JEWS, BY GENERATION (%)

	Generation				
	1	2	3	4	x^2, p. <
Religiously affiliated	93.1	90.3	84.8	94.4	.05
Religiously unaffiliated	34.5	41.7	25.7	19.6	.05
Affiliated (by Index)	77.1	71.7	72.3	81.5	.01
Unaffiliated (by Index)	25.0	39.5	23.0	10.8	.01

TABLE 17

SEDER ATTENDANCE, BY GENERATION (%)

Affiliated With Congregation, Jewish Communal Groups or Both	Participation by Generation			
	1	2	3	4
Yes	85.5	83.1	89.3	81.5
No	51.4	60.5	54.6	37.8
x^2, p. <	.01	.05	.001	.01

Perhaps the most visible form of "passive" Jewish identification is placing a mezuzah on the door frame of a dwelling. Half of Los Angeles Jewry report having a mezuzah on their door frames, with the affiliated more likely to display one, especially in the fourth generation where 69.2% do so. Among fourth generation, high socioeconomic status Jews, 64.7% of the affiliated and 25.0% of the unaffiliated place a mezuzah on their door frames. These various "passive" behaviors appear to be the minimum acceptable level of Jewish identification for large numbers of unaffiliated Jews.

The more generations Los Angeles Jews are removed from their immigrant ancestors, the weaker their religious identity tends to be. However, this decline in identity is not completely transferred to the area of affiliation. Following a drop in the combined rate of religious and communal affiliation from the second to the third generations, there is a rejuvenation in the fourth generation among the great-grandchildren of the immigrants (see Tables 18 and 43). An examination of age categories shows Los Angeles Jews fifty years of age or over much more likely to be affiliated with a congregation and, or, a Jewish communal group than those who are younger (see Table 19), but an assessment of synagogue affiliation alone indicates a decline among those age sixty-five or older (Huberman, 1984).

TABLE 18

AFFILIATION (INDEX), BY GENERATION

	Generation			
Affiliated	1	2	3	4
Yes	57.1	58.2	35.1	42.2
No	42.9	41.8	64.9	57.8
	100.0%	100.0%	100.0%	100.0%

x^2, p. < .01

TABLE 19

AFFILIATION (INDEX), BY AGE

	Age		
Affiliated	Under 30	30-49	50 and over
Yes	35.4	37.9	54.2
No	64.6	62.1	45.8
	100.0%	100.0%	100.0%

x^2, p. $<$ .01

Membership in congregations increases as the income of Los Angeles Jews rises and, when income reaches $40,000 a year or more, there is a much higher likelihood that a family will join a temple or synagogue. The same situation holds when the affiliation index is used, with those families whose incomes are $40,000 a year or over much more likely to be members of Jewish organizations and, or, congregations (see Table 20). But Jewish professionals are less likely to be affiliated or to give to Jewish causes than those in business. It is also important to recognize the contradiction inherent in the fact that the higher the socioeconomic status of Jews, the lower the level of Jewish identity.

Jewish women tend to have a stronger religious identity than men, and they are much more likely to be affiliated with Jewish groups. The Los Angeles data underscore this important difference in rates of affiliation with 23.6% of Jewish men and 33.3% of Jewish women indicating membership in a congregation, and 20.4% of men and 33.3% of women belonging to a non-congregational Jewish group. Women of the third and fourth generations, in particular, are becoming increasingly involved in Jewish institutions and their "return" impacts significantly on organized Jewish life.

TABLE 20

AFFILIATION (CONGREGATION, INDEX), BY FAMILY INCOME (%)

Affiliated	Under $15,000	$15,000 to $39,000	$40,000 And Over	x^2, p. <
Belong to a congregation	19.4	23.3	44.0	.01
Belong according to Affiliation Index	37.0	38.8	58.7	.05

The Jewishness of the neighborhoods in which they grew up does not appear to have had a controlling influence on the affiliation of Jews in Los Angeles. Nonetheless, affiliated Jews today are more likely to perceive the neighborhoods in which they live as Jewish or mixed and to actually live in such places. In terms of the Jewish density of the areas in which Los Angeles Jews now live, 39.0% of the affiliated and 27.5% of the unaffiliated reside in neighborhoods with heavy concentrations of Jews (see Table 21). This suggests that many unaffiliated Jews derive a significant measure of satisfaction from living among other Jews. Indeed, the data show that 36.5% of the unaffiliated and 54.5% of the affiliated wish their neighbors to be Jewish.

Affiliated Jews report that over 80% of their closest friends are Jewish, but the figure drops to just over 60% for the unaffiliated. Both see their friends and talk to them frequently on the telephone, while also maintaining close and supportive ties to their families. The data indicate that 72.6% of the affiliated and 53.0% of the unaffiliated also feel closer to other Jews. Large numbers of Jews are unwilling to express such a preference because it offends their sense of egalitarianism but, in reality, Los Angeles Jews tend to associate with and feel closer to other Jews.

Most Los Angeles Jews, whether affiliated or not, report that their parents were active in or supported Jewish organizations. Those who come from a religious background are somewhat more likely to be affiliated with a congregation, but two-thirds of those who come from a religious home are unaffiliated. At the same time, a considerable number of Los Angeles Jews who did not come from a religious background have chosen to join a synagogue or temple. The personal involvement of parents, especially the father, in regularly attending Sabbath services with the respondent, is also reflected in a higher rate of congregational affiliation.

Patterns of teenage religious observance and participation in Jewish youth groups tend to have a subsequent impact on affiliation. While respondents who were observant in their teens are twice as likely to be affiliated with a congregation, many of the unaffiliated were also observant. Those who were active in Jewish teen groups and who had Jewish friends also have higher rates of affiliation, with a considerable upturn in affiliation from the third to the fourth generations. Both affiliated and unaffiliated respon-

TABLE 21

AFFILIATION (INDEX), BY NEIGHBORHOOD JEWISH DENSITY

	Jewish Density			
Affiliated	Sparse: Under 15 percent	Mixed: 15-44 percent	Heavy: 45 percent or more	Total
Yes	15.9	45.1	39.0	100.0%
No	24.8	47.7	27.5	100.0%

x^2, p. $<$ .05

dents were quite active in non-Jewish teen organizations with no significant differences between these subgroups.

Early and later dating habits are clearly related to patterns of intermarriage as well as to affiliation. Although the affiliated are more likely to date within the group, the evidence shows that most teenage Jews feel free to date non-Jews and there is relatively little parental resistance. A similar pattern has developed among single Jewish adults, both affiliated and unaffiliated, who frequently date people of other faiths, especially in the third and fourth generations (see Table 42). Affiliated Los Angeles Jews of high socioeconomic status show a reversal of the pattern in the fourth generation with 58.8% of this subgroup having always or usually dated other Jews. Among the unaffiliated, fourth generation, high SES, however, only 6.3% always or usually dated within the Jewish group. Differences across generations among unaffiliated Jews of lower socioeconomic status are not statistically significant.

The data indicate that 46.9% of Los Angeles Jews agree synagogue membership is too expensive with 18.6% disagreeing. Both the affiliated and the unaffiliated tend to be in agreement, but resistance to paying dues declines by generation for both. By the fourth generation, only 27.8% of the affiliated and 41.3% of the unaffiliated believe synagogue membership is too expensive. Women and those of low socioeconomic status are the most likely to feel that such costs are excessive. Los Angeles Jews also offer other reasons for not joining a congregation including lack of interest, not religious, and synagogue does not offer programs to meet their needs (Phillips, 1980).

People who have children are members of congregations to a far greater degree than those who are childless. Among Los Angeles Jews, 33.1% of those who have children and only 5.6% of those who do not are affiliated with a temple or synagogue (see Table 22). A rather high proportion believe that synagogue membership should be retained after a child's religious education is completed. The data indicate that 58.4% hold this view, with the religiously affiliated almost twice as likely as the unaffiliated to be in agreement. This attitude toward congregational membership remains high across generations, but the affiliated of the fourth generation show a stronger interest than any other subgroup. It is clear, however, that a significant gap exists between interest in organized religious life and actual membership in a congregation.

Support for Israel and world Jewry is extremely high for both affiliated and unaffiliated Jews in Los Angeles. Many plan to send their children to programs in Israel, especially young people, those of high socioeconomic status, and the affiliated. Israel is seen as a source of strength and pride by over 80% of Los Angeles Jewry, as a spiritual and cultural center by almost 70%, and as an insurance policy by more than one-third. Still, fewer than 4% of the Jews in Los Angeles say they are personally planning to emigrate to Israel, and only 9% feel strongly that Jewish youth should be encouraged to make this decision. Although the affiliated tend to be somewhat more committed to Israel, the differences between them and the unaffiliated are not substantial and are sometimes almost non-existent (see Table 23).

TABLE 22

RELIGIOUS AFFILIATION, BY HAVING CHILDREN

	Have Children	
Affiliated With Congregation	No	Yes
Yes	5.6	33.1
No	94.4	66.9
	100.0%	100.0%

x^2, $p. < .05$

Perhaps more than most large communities, the Jews of Los Angeles have been affected by the significant motivity of American and world society. Even after they arrived, the processes of change continued as they shifted residences and neighborhoods within the metropolitan area. Nonetheless, almost half of the Jews of Los Angeles have established themselves as part of the organized Jewish community through memberships in religious and communal insti-

TABLE 23

AFFILIATION (INDEX), BY ZIONIST MEMBERSHIP, PLANS FOR ALIYAH, VISITING ISRAEL, AND PERSONAL ATTITUDES TOWARD ISRAEL (%)

Affiliated	Israel Insurance Policy	Israel Source of Strength and Pride	Has Visited Israel	Plans to Visit Israel	Plans Aliyah	Ever Been Zionist
Yes	43.2	89.0	36.9	34.1	6.0	24.6
No	28.8	74.8	22.3	21.2	2.2	11.2
x^2, p. <	.01	.001	.01	.01	.05	.001

tutions. They have identified with synagogues, neighborhood and voluntary groups, and other communal structures which are the principal expressions of their Jewish values and concerns. This reassertion of Jewish continuity has also helped them to deal with their most profound human and social needs by offering a communal system that often acts as an extended family during times of personal crisis as well as during happy occasions.

For a number of reasons, more than half of the Los Angeles Jewish population has not affiliated with the organized Jewish community. Some are apathetic or indifferent to synagogue or organizational life, while others feel unwelcome or are priced out of the institutional complex. There are those who are insecure and uncomfortable with their Jewish identity, factors that contribute to the processes of assimilation. But there is also an upturn of interest among many Los Angeles Jews, especially among the great-grandchildren of the immigrants, young people who are becoming more intensively Jewish and religious and more interested in learning about their Jewish identity. This resurgence of commitment is acted out both through affiliation with Jewish religious and communal institutions, as well as by a search for new, less formal, and more personally satisfying Jewish environments.

IV

Culture and Education

Jewish tradition places emphasis upon mastery of the Jewish cultural heritage as one means of forming a sound identity. The Jews of Los Angeles have a strong reservoir of commitment to Jewish cultural expression, manifested by their interest in Jewish educational and cultural institutions, Jewish periodicals, books, music, and the language and history of the Jewish people. There is also general acceptance of the view that children should have some Jewish education that will help to shape their values and behavior as well as to influence the transmission of Jewishness to future generations.

Culture is an essential part of the human endowment and has a profound impact upon the development of a personal identity. An individual's culture includes a particular set of values, beliefs, and practices usually passed down from generation to generation and exercising a powerful influence on behavior. Through language as well as by example, the culture in which one is raised affects the growth of personality and helps one to adapt to the environment (Lidz, 1968).

It took long periods of time for Jewish culture to blossom in other diaspora societies including Babylon, Spain, and Poland, and the processes of cultural development may well be in their earliest stages in this country. American Jews of different generations are now engaged in a multiplicity of cultural activities aimed at strengthening group cohesiveness and Jewish identity. Significant investments of creative energy and financial resources are being made in various forms of Jewish education because Jewish leaders have generally accepted the view that cultural awareness and knowledge are central ingredients in the future of Jewish life.

In the early days of Los Angeles Jewish settlement, Jews brought with them the tradition of Jewish education together with its methods and institutions. At first there were private schools or tutors, but late in the nineteenth century synagogues were sponsoring programs of Jewish education. By the second generation, parents turned increasingly to Jewish schools to socialize their children in the values, traditions, and culture of the Jewish people. The rate of attendance accelerated after World War II with more than half of Jewish children receiving some kind of Jewish education, so that the schools took over many of the educational functions of the family.

Since World War II, Los Angeles Jews have been moving out to the "suburbs" and congregating in voluntary neighborhood and psychological enclaves. They join synagogues "for the sake of the children" and seek the educational facilities and rites of passage available through them including bar mitzvah, bat mitzvah, and confirmation. This attachment to the synagogue often ends as the children grow up, and these families are replaced by others with younger children. Increased norms of attendance and participation are established as prerequisites for bar mitzvah, and some parents are upset because of the additional burden on already heavy schedules. The problem is exacerbated when children are encouraged to participate in rituals and observance greater than existing home patterns (Sidorsky, 1973).

One of the difficulties educators face is the assumption that young Jews come to school with a commitment to Judaism or at least a considerable degree of self-awareness as Jews. That assumption no longer holds since most arrive at school without adequate Jewish commitment or identification (Silberman, 1975). In addition, many young Jews in Los Angeles are asking not how they can be more Jewish but, rather, why they should be Jewish at all. The limited Jewish behavior of their parents is reinforced by the kind of freedom of choice that enables young people to press for relevant answers.

Total Jewish school enrollment has declined significantly in the past two decades according to a national census taken by the American Association for Jewish Education (*Jewish Telegraphic Agency*, Nov. 7, 1979). Most children are enrolled in a Jewish school between the ages of eight and twelve, but the number declines sharply after the rites of bar and bat mitzvah. The number of Jewish children in Hebrew schools has dropped well below 400,000, but it is estimated that by 1990 the children of the post-war babies should provide an increase in Hebrew school enrollment (Yaffe, 1980).

Jewish educators and community leaders are responding to these concerns by seeking a more comprehensive educational process that involves both the cognitive development of the individual and the climate of interpersonal relations that helps to foster more positive Jewish attitudes and behavior among young people. It is now recognized that Jewish education in isolation of other related elements cannot be effective and lasting in its impact on Jewish intellectual and emotional growth. Family, peer, and community factors contribute materially to a positive and supportive environment for the Jewish education of children.

There are different kinds of Jewish schools today including elementary and secondary all-day schools, a variety of supplementary elementary and secondary schools, and Jewish preschools. In addition to Orthodox, Conservative, Reform, and Reconstructionist institutions of higher education, there are Jewish studies programs at universities and a host of adult education activities. The three major types of Jewish schools are the weekday afternoon school, the one-day-a-week Sunday school, and the day school, with the preponderance of students enrolled in supplementary Jewish education.

A substantial proportion of Jewish parents are committed to the public schools, so that the great majority of Jewish children in Los Angeles receive their Jewish education in afternoon, evening, or weekend schools. Most graduates of three-day-a-week supplementary schools have little recognizable fluency in Hebrew and cannot understand more than carefully edited texts based on a limited vocabulary; the Sunday schools are even worse in terms of academic achievement (Ackerman, 1973). Moreover, according to the executive director of the Bureau of Jewish Education, about 40% have been exposed to no Jewish education at all (*Los Angeles Times*, October 13, 1984).

Day school graduates seem to be much more knowledgable than those of other schools if a knowledge of traditional Jewish texts is used as a criterion of the educated youth. As a private institution with a strong religious orientation, the day school offers instruction in Jewish studies as well as the general subjects of the public school. Although sometimes thought of as parochial schools, many are not under the control of congregations. There has been considerable resistance to day schools stemming from the belief that they inhibit opportunities for full participation in American life, but they are increasingly accepted and there is now at least one such school in every city with a Jewish population of over 7,500.

The growth of Jewish day school enrollment is fed by a search for Jewish roots, concern for better education, and the continued influx of newcomers to Los Angeles. Reflecting a nationwide trend in Jewish education, there are currently twenty-four Jewish day schools in Los Angeles, most on the west side and in the San Fernando Valley. Much of the growth stems from new schools linked with the Conservative and Reform movements, but Orthodox day schools are also expanding as a result of the inflow of strictly observant families as well as their higher birth rates. Although many parents are concerned with the high cost of day school education, there are now well over 5,000 day schoolers who comprise about a quarter of the children presently receiving a Jewish education.

Studies suggest that the type of Jewish education does not especially affect the extent of affiliation, but the quantity of Jewish education appears to be the critical factor in the development of a strong sense of Jewishness (Bock, 1977 and Huberman, 1984). The number of hours of Jewish instruction is especially important as a predictive measure of Jewish identification and participation (H. Himmelfarb, 1974). In a day school program, Judaica is taught from twelve to twenty hours a week for up to forty weeks a year, with a six-year Jewish education varying from 2,700 to 4,800 hours. Supplementary Jewish education is far more limited, so that the total time spent over eight years can vary from 1,000 hours to 2,000 or more, especially if the student goes on to a supplementary Hebrew high school. Those who have spent significantly more hours in Jewish classrooms are usually more religious, more involved in Jewish social networks, more knowledgable about Jewish culture, and more likely to be involved in non-congregational Jewish organizational activities.

In studying the Jewish identity and behavior of Los Angeles Jews, a Jewish education index was constructed to differentiate the respondents in terms of the quantities of their Jewish education. An assessment of the distribution of responses indicated that those with at least six years of Jewish all-day school or eight or more years each of supplementary and Sunday school could be considered as having a heavy Jewish education. Of those who responded, and most did, only 8.2% had a heavy Jewish education, 49.2% a moderate one, and 42.6% little or none. What the data indicate is that a total of 1,000 hours of Jewish education is the very minimum threshold of meaningful impact on Jewish attitudes and behavior (Bock, 1977), but Los Angeles Jews and their children who are mostly products of limited supplementary Jewish education do not usually achieve even this minimum time exposure.

Young people in Los Angeles receive a Jewish education that is largely under synagogue auspices with the schools providing an intellectual content of ideas and practices including a knowledge of classical Jewish texts, commitment to the study of Torah, and facility in Hebrew language and literature. Other objectives are the encouragement of identification with the Jewish people and its future throughout the world, understanding the unique place of Israel, and inculcating faith in God. There is also a growing acceptance of the view that educational influences are exerted by the conscious awareness of the relationship between Jewish tradition and democracy that points up the compatibility of Judaism and the American ethic.

But Jewish education today is not always effective in strengthening commitment to Jewish values or identification because the goals and practices of some schools do not reflect the radically different environments confronting Jews at this time. The problem cannot be blamed entirely on the schools, however, since it is difficult to teach children values and knowledge without the support and commitment of their parents (Ackerman, 1969 and Gordis, 1974). Moreover, educators are asked to carry out their responsibilities in the face of a decline in the amount of time available to teach those who receive a Jewish education (Hochberg, 1972).

A related concern is that Jewish education is largely supplementary, with teachers not generally employed on a full-time basis, inadequately paid, and with limited training. Many of the teachers are Israelis or Yeshiva graduates who may have difficulty in communicating with children from different backgrounds. Jewish schools have also suffered from financial problems and inflation even though tuition fees and allocations from community funds have increased.

Nonetheless, there are clear indications that Jewish education does have some impact on the attitudes and behavior of Los Angeles Jews. The data generated in this study show that those who have had a strong Jewish education are the most committed to maintaining synagogue membership after their children's religious education has been completed, followed by the moderately educated, and those who have had little or none. The heavily educated are four times as likely as all others to prefer day schools for their children, while supplementary and Sunday schools attract the most interest from individuals who have had a moderate Jewish education. But there is little difference between those who had a moderate or strong Jewish education regarding whether or not their parents forced them to attend religious services when they were young (see Table 24).

Religiously affiliated Jews tend to accumulate a stronger Jewish education than the unaffiliated, but many Jewishly educated persons belong to no Jewish groups at all. By the fourth generation, even among the affiliated, relatively few have had a good Jewish education, and more than one-third of those who belong to a synagogue have had little or none. Orthodox Jews are the most likely to have had a significant Jewish education, Conservative Jews a moderate one, and Reform Jews less.

Jewish education has always been viewed as a major factor in the creation of a strong Jewish identity, and this is reflected in the religious, cultural, and national (peoplehood) identity scores measured by the scales developed for this study. There is a clear association between a strong Jewish education and a powerful sense of Jewish peoplehood, and a good Jewish education also influences the development of a strong Jewish religious identity. But a rather large proportion of Jews who have had only a moderate Jewish education or even none also manifest considerable religiosity.

There is a direct association between the Jewish cultural identity of Los Angeles Jews and the quantity of their Jewish education, with those who are the highest scorers on the cultural identity subscale tending to have the greatest amount of Jewish education. There is a considerable degree of Jewish cultural identity among Jews who have received a moderate or even a little Jewish education, suggesting that other factors may also influence the formation of a positive Jewish identity (see Table 25).

The cultural behavior of parents in the home environment exer-

TABLE 24

CHILD'S JEWISH EDUCATION AND SYNAGOGUE PARTICIPATION, BY JEWISH EDUCATION (%)

	Jewish Education Index			
	Little or None	Moderate	Strong	x^2, p. <
Plans to send child to afternoon Jewish school	45.8	64.2	44.0	.01
Plans to send child to Sunday school	49.6	69.1	28.0	.001
Plans to send child to parochial (all-day) school	8.5	7.4	28.0	.01
Should maintain synagogue membership after child's religious education is completed	49.1	61.3	80.6	.01
Parents forced me to attend religious services	12.7	32.6	32.3	.001

cises a profound influence on the growth of personality with children adapting to the ways of those who raise them. This is especially important in the creation of a cultural identity as parents impact on the transmission of Jewish practices and beliefs. In the context of the home milieu, the child usually learns the distinctive customs of the Jewish heritage as well as those that have been acquired from the general culture.

TABLE 25

JEWISH CULTURAL IDENTITY SCORES, BY JEWISH EDUCATION

	Jewish Education		
Cultural Identity	Little or None	Moderate	Strong
Low	57.1	50.6	26.7
High	42.9	49.4	73.3
	100.0%	100.0%	100.0%

x^2, p. < .01

The schools are also part of the continuum of educational experiences and cultural activities that take place throughout the life cycle with no one point necessarily more important than any other. Adult education is as useful as educating elementary and secondary school children, and camp experiences and work in Israel are also significant in the life-long education of Jews (Ackerman, 1973). Alternative programs are particularly important in fostering a meaningful commitment to Jewish life especially among children from the ages of eight to thirteen (American Jewish Committee, 1976).

While many in Los Angeles are Jewishly ignorant, there is widespread recognition of the importance of Jewish supplementary and day schools, adult education courses, and Jewish studies programs in colleges and universities. A significant proportion of Los Angeles Jews read books on Jewish subjects, subscribe to newspapers and journals that discuss Jewish issues, and support scholarship in higher Jewish education. Los Angeles Jews of different generations are engaged in a multiplicity of Jewish cultural activities including support for Jewish historical societies, museums, and libraries. Thousands are exposed to Jewish radio and television programs, while synagogues, centers, and other groups devote themselves to the study of Hebrew, Yiddish, visits to Israel, and other aspects of the Jewish cultural experience.

A considerable proportion of Los Angeles Jews continue their Jewish learning throughout the life cycle. The data show that approximately one-quarter of the Jewish population has taken some adult Jewish courses, especially those with the heaviest early Jewish education who are also the most inclined to read books on Jewish topics, local Jewish newspapers, and Jewish magazines. But those with more limited amounts of Jewish education also show some disposition to Jewish learning, and many enroll in adult courses and partake of various kinds of Jewish reading (see Table 26).

There has been a steady erosion in the use of Yiddish and Hebrew, but data collected by the U.S. Census Bureau (1972) indicate that almost 1,600,000 Jews in the U.S. declare Yiddish their mother tongue. Of these over 400,000 are foreign born, almost 1,000,000 second generation, and nearly 200,000 third generation. Today, many young Jews are becoming familiar with Yiddish and Hebrew in recognition of the meaning of language to Jewish identity and continuity. Still, only 31.0% of Los Angeles Jews know Yiddish well and 34.0% a little. As for Hebrew, 10.4% have a good grasp of the language and 29.8% a little. Understanding of Hebrew increases with the amount of Jewish education including adult courses, but there is no significant difference with respect to Yiddish probably because it is studied far less than Hebrew.

Los Angeles Jews with the strongest Jewish education are the most likely to have had a bar or bat mitzvah, but confirmation is more prevalent among those with a moderate Jewish education. Only 35.4% of Los Angeles Jews have had a bar or bat mitzvah and

TABLE 26

JEWISH READING HABITS, BY JEWISH EDUCATION (%)

	Jewish Education Index			
	Little or None	Moderate	Strong	x^2, p. <
Frequently, occasionally reads books on Jewish topics	65.8	77.5	80.0	.05
Frequently, occasionally reads local Jewish newspapers	40.0	50.5	67.7	.01
Frequently, occasionally reads Jewish magazines	31.1	45.4	63.3	.001
Has taken one or more adult Jewish education courses	18.0	28.1	38.7	.05

fewer, 24.9%, have been confirmed. Still, most Jewish parents see bar or bat mitzvah as a major aspect of the education of their children, even while the religious example set in their homes is limited. Parents are more interested in encouraging a bar mitzvah for their sons than a bat mitzvah for their daughters, especially the Orthodox who tend to see the bar mitzvah as a central element in the Jewish maturation of their male children. Interest in the bar mitzvah increases with the quantity of the respondent's own Jewish education (see Table 27), but there is little difference among Los Angeles Jews with respect to daughters having a bat mitzvah.

There is increasing difficulty in encouraging children to study Jewishly and to carry on the traditions that their parents have ignored. On the other hand, there is a clear association between the positive Jewish behaviors of parents and the ways in which these have been extended in the Jewish education of their children. Respondents whose parents were religiously observant or who supported Jewish organizations are the most likely to have had a strong Jewish education. Their parents were more observant in lighting Sabbath candles, buying kosher meat, and using separate dishes. Those whose fathers attended services with them are especially likely to have had a good Jewish education, and the influence of mothers is also significant. With respect to the fasting of parents on Yom Kippur, this is associated with both a moderate and a strong Jewish education among their children. As would be expected, Los Angeles Jews with the least Jewish education are the most likely to have experienced a Christmas tree in the home of their parents (see Table 28).

Those Jews who have had the most Jewish education are not necessarily the strongest supporters of Israel, and a differential pattern emerges on certain key indicators. The most Jewishly educated are far more likely to have been members of a Zionist organization and to encourage the aliyah of American youth. But in regard to seeing Israel as a source of strength and pride and trying to influence U.S. support on behalf of the State, individuals with a moderate Jewish education express even more support that those who have had more, with the lowest educated group not far behind in these views (see Table 29). It is particularly noteworthy that Los Angeles Jews with a moderate Jewish education are the most inclined to support the United Jewish Welfare Fund.

The Jewishly educated are the most opposed to having women as

TABLE 27

BAR/BAT MITZVAH, CONFIRMATION, BY JEWISH EDUCATION (%)

	Jewish Education Index			
	Little or None	Moderate	Strong	x^2, p. <
Had bar/bat mitzvah	18.1	45.7	67.6	.001
Was confirmed	9.4	38.6	29.0	.001
Sons should have bar mitzvah	60.2	73.7	80.6	.01

TABLE 28

OBSERVANCE OF PARENTS, BY RESPONDENT'S JEWISH EDUCATION (%)

Behaviors of Parents (Always, Usually)	Jewish Education Index			
	Little or None	Moderate	Strong	x^2, p. <
Home religiously observant	29.7	44.0	61.3	.001
Active in or supported Jewish organizations	36.2	69.3	77.4	.001
Lighted Sabbath candles	46.2	70.1	80.6	.001
Bought kosher meat	55.3	70.2	93.5	.001
Used separate dishes	29.1	40.8	77.4	.001
Fasted on Yom Kippur	60.1	89.1	87.1	.001
Father attended Sabbath services with me	29.9	63.8	83.3	.001
Mother attended Sabbath services with me	27.8	61.0	66.7	.001
Parents had a Christmas tree	30.0	15.8	3.3	.001

TABLE 29

SUPPORT FOR ISRAEL, BY JEWISH EDUCATION (%)

	Jewish Education Index			
	Little or None	Moderate	Strong	x^2, p. <
Should encourage Jewish youth to emigrate to Israel	24.2	30.2	53.3	.01
Israel is a source of strength and pride	72.6	87.3	80.6	.01
Has ever been a member of a Zionist organization	6.3	15.8	48.4	.001
U.S. Jews should try to influence American policy for Israel	75.8	87.8	83.9	.05

rabbis or in minyans, and are more inclined than others to see themselves as part of a national, cultural, or ethnic group than as members of a religious community. Their psychological security comes into question since they are the most Jewishly sensitive as measured by indicators assessing the exposure of their Jewishness to non-Jews. There is little difference among the Jewish educational subgroups regarding the impact of growing up in a Jewish neighborhood, the quantity of their secular education or levels of socioeconomic status. And persons with the least Jewish education tend to see their relatives more often, which suggests that some of their Jewish needs are met in the psycho-social environments of kinship.

The data indicate that large numbers of Los Angeles Jews have been significantly deprived with respect to Jewish languages, history, and culture. For many, supplementary congregational schools have become symbols of Jewishness as parents transfer responsibility to others for their children's education with little personal involvement or support. It is not surprising, therefore, that Jewish children are not particularly interested in a Jewish educational process that does not reflect the attitudes and behavior of most of their parents. Moreover, the amount of time spent in acquiring a Jewish education is usually so small as to have minimal effect.

Jewish identity can be strengthened by what is learned in Jewish schools if sufficient time is given to the process and if the educational and family environments help to create an emotional commitment to the values and beliefs of the group. While this generation of young Jews has received a Jewish education from more qualified teachers using better educational materials, there has been only limited success in training them for a positive and happy acceptance of their Jewishness. In response to this challenge, Jewish scholarly efforts have grown in importance within the Los Angeles Jewish community. A cadre of volunteer and professional leadership is committed to Jewish intellectual excellence through strengthening and expanding Jewish education.

The University of Judaism, the Hebrew Union College/Jewish Institute of Religion, and Yeshiva University are effectively training increasing numbers of teachers, rabbis, and Jewish communal workers. Jewish studies programs are growing at UCLA and other universities so that the college campus now offers many young Jews their first serious encounter with Jewish education. More and more Jewish scholars are teaching Hebrew, Yiddish, Jewish literature, history, Talmud, philosophy, and sociology and, increasingly, synagogues and centers are offering Jewish adult education courses. All of these efforts are reinforced by Jewish historical groups, book and music programs, and numerous activities focused on various aspects of Jewish culture.

The American Association for Jewish Education, the American Jewish Committee, and national education commissions within each of the denominations are conducting research, developing curricular materials, and establishing standards. The Bureau of Jewish Education in Los Angeles is even closer to the schools and, as additional funds are made available, they are experimenting with innovative educational modes, along with seminars, in-service training, development of libraries, testing and placement services, and publication activities. This is reinforced by a growing movement toward more relevant themes such as Holocaust courses, materials dealing with Israel, Soviet Jewry, and the American Jewish community, as well as the use of new textbooks and programs for teaching the Bible, history, holidays, and Hebrew. But the work in curriculum reform still deals with pieces of curriculum rather than its entirety, while the need is to integrate educational techniques and Jewish values so that children will learn how to function in Jewish environments (Gordis, 1974 and H. Himmelfarb, 1975).

V

Jewish Peoplehood

The fluidity of the Los Angeles environment has created opportunities for varied expressions of Jewish religious and communal behavior. In a community culture that recognizes the individual's right of personal decision, self-identification has often been the critical element in determining who is a Jew and how this Jewishness should be expressed. In this setting, Jews have been able themselves to define the extent to which they wish to be Jewish without the traditional pressures of family or community. This has had very powerful implications for the changing character of Jewish identity among the Jews of Los Angeles.

Jewish identification is undergirded by Jewish law which suggests that all who are born Jews are considered Jewish, but there are differences in Israel and the diaspora on the question of who is a Jew. Israel's Law of Return is being debated in the context of an attempt to define the word "Jew" solely according to Jewish religious law, with those who hold the most traditional view demanding total adherence to precise traditional requirements. Los Angeles Jews, particularly Conservative and Reform, have objected to a proposed amendment to the Law of Return, believing it would weaken Jewish religious pluralism and bring into question the Jewish identity of many converts to Judaism and their children.

Jewish identity is difficult to define because there are so many different kinds of Jews ranging from religious to secular, from Jews in Israel to Jews in the diaspora, from those who are Jews by commitment to those who have assimilated, and from those who are Jews all of the time to those who are Jews occasionally. There are aspects of the Jewish experience, however, that are applicable to all Jews and can facilitate understanding of the nature of Jewish identity. Jews can be characterized by a sense of peoplehood focused on Israel, responses to the meaning of the Holocaust, or merely the fact of claiming to be Jewish.

Jews also define themselves in psychological and sociological terms, finding new ways to respond to their political, social, cultural, and family life as well as their occupational choices, social mobility, and status. They seek psychological comfort in being Jews and engaging in Jewish practices because of their psychic needs rather than obedience to divine commands. With them it feels good to be Jewish and to do things with other Jews. For many, "the recent increase in Jewish participation stems from a search for Jewish adjustment rather than a return to belief in God, and ethnicity and group membership are increasingly important" (Bubis, 1980).

All that happened to Jews in the past and is happening today helps to shape the definition of what is Jewish. Various areas of Jewish identification are intertwined so that the most identified Jews tend to be active in several aspects of Jewish life. Those with higher levels of Jewish identity join in activities and have attitudes that pertain to attendance at religious services, membership in Jewish organizations, work for Israel, and concern over children's Jewish education. A majority of Jews, however, even those involved in the same areas of activity, do so with a considerably lower degree of participation. Consequently, the Los Angeles Jewish community must be defined as something larger than its formal institutions.

There is an ongoing commitment to Jewish peoplehood, ingroup loyalty, and communal obligation among Los Angeles Jews. This is reflected in a sense of kinship and group identification that is acted out through family and friendship patterns as well as a concern with the survival of the Jewish people. The changing dimensions of Jewish life in Los Angeles are further indicated by the dramatic shift from religious to ethnic and cultural identification with its profound implications for defining who is a Jew. Today, relatively few Los Angeles Jews say the quality that best describes Jews is "religious," with most choosing "ethnic-cultural" as a defining characteristic.

Jewish identification has moved from religion, language, and institutions to the social, economic, and ethnic interests of the group. Jews are deeply involved with their own group concerns and are increasingly willing to express their views in the political and communal environments. They are committed to the fight against anti-Semitism in this country and abroad and speak out vigorously when Jews are victimized by discrimination or persecution. Expressions of interdependence and ingroup responsibility are manifested in a variety of ways ranging from political action, to voting for sympathetic candidates, to public demonstrations on behalf of Soviet Jewry.

Changes taking place among Jews in Los Angeles were measured by the Jewish identity scale (see Table 30). Analysis of the data shows a more or less straight line decline of Jewish identity among Los Angeles Jews from the first through the third generations, a pattern that is consistent with earlier findings on ethnic groups (Sandberg, 1974 and Warner, 1953). There is, however, a leveling off of the decline and some upturn of identity from the third to the fourth generations (see Table 31). Other attitudinal and behavioral indicators also point to a selective renaissance of Jewish interest in the fourth generation.

The first generation, the immigrant group, has the strongest Jewish identity, but the difference between the first and second generations is less than expected. An ethnic resurgence has taken place among all generations, particularly the second, stimulated in large measure by the Black Power movement of the 1960s and the new acceptance of ethnic identification. The Los Angeles data also suggest that the third and fourth generations are similar in terms of Jewish identity and that there is a reservoir of strong Jewish feeling in these generations. Further analysis of a number of key items in the study points to an ethnic-cultural upturn among fourth generation Los Angeles Jews. These are the great-grandchildren of the immigrants who have had little if any direct exposure to the immigrant culture.

Table 32 presents a graphic view of the differences of mean levels of Jewish identity as measured by the various identity subscales across generations. National identity (peoplehood) is the strongest of the three subconstructs, followed by cultural and then religious identity. After a decline from the first to the third generations, national and cultural identity show an upturn. Religious identity declines across generations in a more or less straight line, with the communal aspects of religion somewhat stronger than the devotional.

The relative fluidity of America's social class system allows for

TABLE 30

JEWISH IDENTITY SCALE

Strongly disagree	Moderately disagree	Disagree	Agree	Moderately agree	Strongly agree
1	2	3	4	5	6

Items 1-10: Cultural

1. The public schools should teach more about the contribution of Jews to America.
2. Organizations which carry on the Jewish culture are not very important.
3. Los Angeles newspapers should feature more news about Jewish community life.
4. We need to know the history of the Jewish people.
5. We should be willing to give money to preserve our Jewish heritage.
6. It is too bad that the Jewish tradition is not being carried on by more of our young people.
7. Jews should read Jewish periodicals and books.
8. I like to listen to Jewish music.
9. Jewish education is essential for Jewish survival.
10. It is not important for American Jews to learn Hebrew.

Items 11-20: National

11. A Jewish neighborhood is a friendlier place to live.
12. It is all right to change your name.
13. I feel more comfortable with Jewish people.
14. It is better for a Jew to marry someone who is Jewish.

TABLE 30

JEWISH IDENTITY SCALE *(Continued)*

Strongly disagree	Moderately disagree	Disagree	Agree	Moderately agree	Strongly agree
1	2	3	4	5	6

15. I feel an obligation to help Jews anywhere in the world who are in need.
16. You can be for your own people first and still be a good American.
17. It is not important for Jews to continue as a people.
18. It is important to encourage a sense of Jewish identification in our children.
19. I am glad I was born a Jew.
20. I feel no special bonds to the state of Israel.

Items 21-25: Religious Communal

21. It is important for me to contribute my time and resources to a synagogue or temple.
22. I like attending religious services to be with other Jews.
23. I enjoy participating in synagogue programs.
24. Pesach Seders are important to me.
25. Our religious tradition helps to bring Jewish people closer together.

Items 26-30: Religious Devotional

26. Attending services on the High Holy Days is important for me.
27. Jewish prayers help me when I am troubled.
28. I feel good when the Sabbath candles are lighted.
29. I am moved when I hear the Shofar (ram's horn).
30. The Jewish faith is a source of real strength to me.

TABLE 31

MEAN LEVELS OF TOTAL JEWISH IDENTITY, BY GENERATION

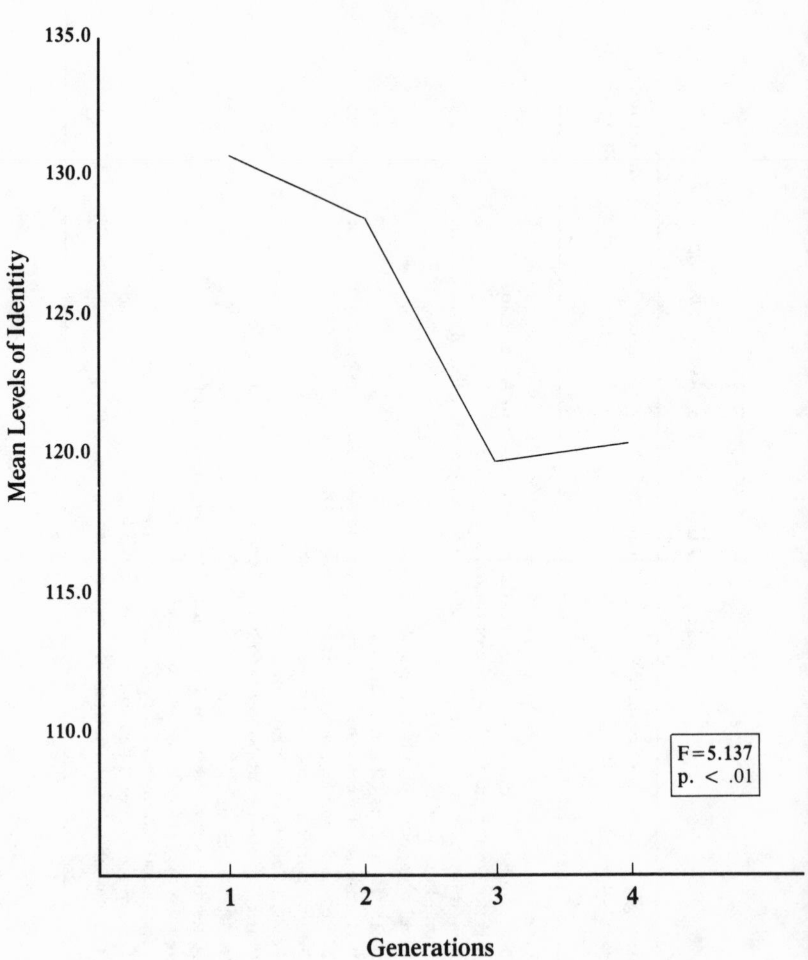

TABLE 32

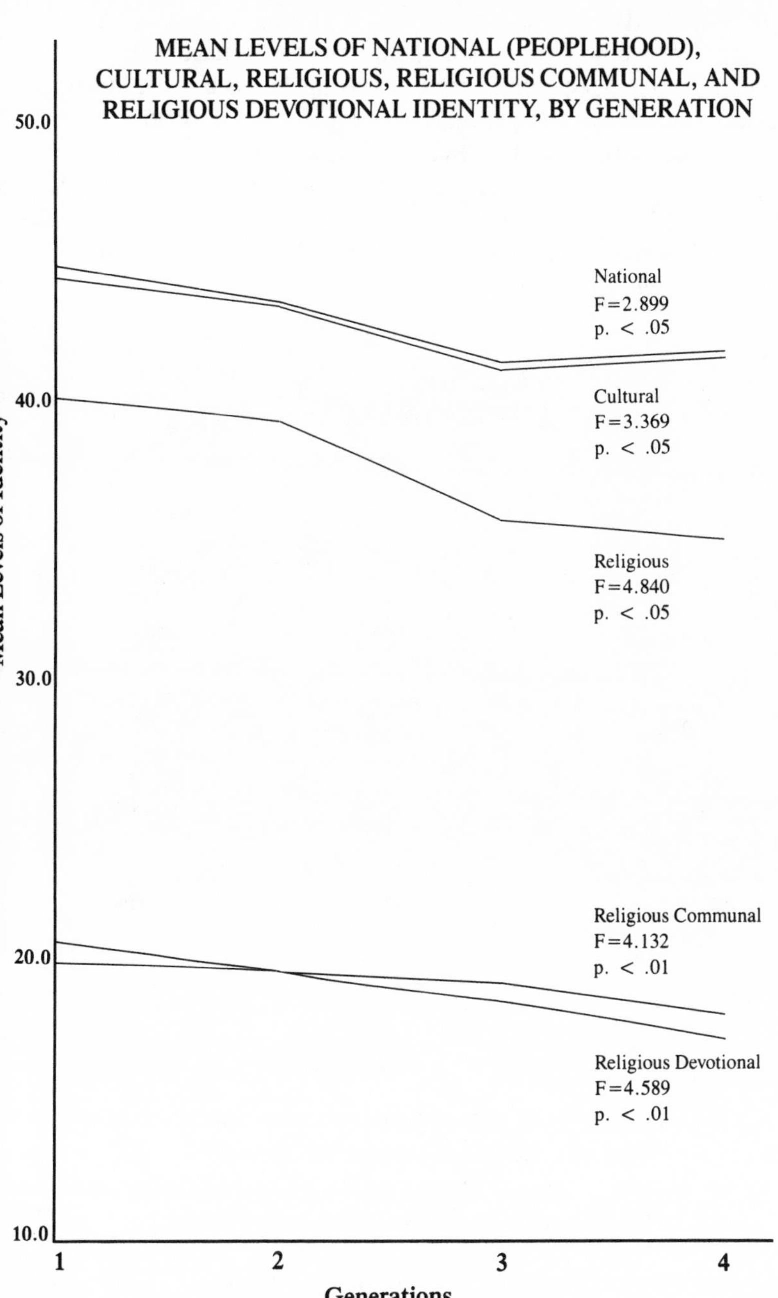
MEAN LEVELS OF NATIONAL (PEOPLEHOOD), CULTURAL, RELIGIOUS, RELIGIOUS COMMUNAL, AND RELIGIOUS DEVOTIONAL IDENTITY, BY GENERATION
Mean Levels of Identity
50.0
40.0
30.0
20.0
10.0
National
F=2.899
p. < .05
Cultural
F=3.369
p. < .05
Religious
F=4.840
p. < .05
Religious Communal
F=4.132
p. < .01
Religious Devotional
F=4.589
p. < .01
1
2
3
4
Generations

the upward mobility of Jews and others, a process that has been highly disruptive to the various ethnic groups seeking to maintain some holding power over their members. The relatedness of ethnic identity and socioeconomic factors was analyzed in order to facilitate examination of the hypothesis that the Jewish identity of those who are upwardly mobile tends to decline. An assessment of the data suggests there are clear differences between Los Angeles Jews of high and low socioeconomic status and that those who have risen in affluence and social position tend to have a weaker Jewish identity (see Table 33).

TABLE 33

JEWISH IDENTITY SCORES,
BY SOCIOECONOMIC STATUS

	SES Groups	
Jewish Identity	Low	High
Low	40.7	55.3
High	59.3	44.7
	100.0%	100.0%

x^2, p. < .05

Data generated from the national identity subconstruct of the Jewish identity scale show that a sense of peoplehood holds steady from the second to the fourth generations among Los Angeles Jews, following a decline from the first to the second generations. The sex of the respondents also appears to be of importance in the analysis of Jewish identity. As a group, Los Angeles Jewish women have a stronger Jewish identity than men, with 58.0% of the female respondents having high Jewish identity scores as compared with only 44.8% of the males (see Table 34). The data elsewhere in this volume support the view that women tend to be more affirmatively Jewish than men.

TABLE 34

HIGH SCORERS ON JEWISH IDENTITY SCALE, BY GENDER, PARENT'S OBSERVANCE, AND TEEN OBSERVANCE (%)

	Male	Female	x^2, p. <
Gender	44.8	58.0	.05
	Observant	Not Observant	
Observance of parent's home	62.5	43.8	.001
	Observant	Not Observant	
Teenage observance	60.2	32.5	.001

Jewish education has traditionally stimulated the formation of Jewish identity by transmitting the values, beliefs, language, and history of the Jewish people. Together with family, community, and societal influences, Jewish education contributes to the emergence of a personal self-definition in an ongoing process of group socialization. As indicated earlier, the Jews of Los Angeles have had varying degrees of Jewish education, and those with the greatest quantity usually have the strongest Jewish identities. Among those with a strong Jewish education, 79.3% have high Jewish identity scores; 54.0% of those with a moderate Jewish education have high identity scores; and there is a decline to 40.6% among those with little or no Jewish education. Some Los Angeles Jews with a strong

Jewish identity have had little or no Jewish education, while others with a weak identity have had considerable education. This supports the notion that Jewish education is only one factor in the formation of Jewish identity (see Table 35).

TABLE 35

JEWISH IDENTITY SCORES, BY JEWISH EDUCATION

	Jewish Education Index		
Jewish Identity	Little or None	Moderate	Strong
Low	59.4	46.0	20.7
High	40.6	54.0	79.3
	100.0%	100.0%	100.0%

x^2, p. $< .001$

The strength of an individual's Jewish identity is an important factor in the decision to join a congregation, and Los Angeles Jews with high Jewish identity scores are more than three times as likely to be religiously affiliated than those with low scores. The ratio declines to two to one among Jews who belong to non-congregational Jewish groups. This means that a strong Jewish identity is more likely to be associated with religious than communal affiliation. Nonetheless, many Los Angeles Jews with a strong Jewish identity are unaffiliated with a congregation or other Jewish organization (see Table 36).

The importance of coming from a religiously observant home is often cited as a factor in the formation of a positive Jewish identity. This appears to be generally true for the Jews of Los Angeles but the picture is far from clear. Among those who come from a religiously observant home, 62.5% have a strong Jewish identity as compared with 43.8% from non-observant homes who also have a strong Jewish identity. The fact that many Jews who are from observant backgrounds score low on the Jewish identity scale suggests that coming from an observant home is only one element in the creation of a positive Jewish identity (see Table 34).

TABLE 36

JEWISH IDENTITY SCORES, BY AFFILIATION (%)

	Jewish Institutions		
Jewish Identity	Religious	Communal	Both
Low	14.0	19.7	29.2
High	44.1	37.0	61.4
x^2, p. <	.001	.001	.001

A number of social scientists and educators have commented on the significance of teenage behavior as a critical component in the formation of Jewish identity. One of the more important factors mentioned in this analysis is the association between teenage observance and the development of a wholesome Jewish identity. The data for Jews in Los Angeles show the existence of a relationship with 60.2% of those who were observant as teenagers having high Jewish identity scores as compared with 32.5% of those who were not observant (see Table 34). It is clear that early patterns of observance make a difference for many, but a considerable number of those who were observant in their teen years have a weak Jewish identity.

The subject of Jewish identity is often discussed in terms of ethnicity, a relatively new term that goes beyond belonging to a particular ethnic group and embodies the search for ethnic pride and rootedness. Ethnicity has been interpreted as relating to a common culture, territory of residence, and a historically distinct population, but it also involves the self-conscious action of those who seek to shape their own lives in terms of their unique values, traditions, and interests.

Ethnic identity and ethnicity are used to describe various aspects of Jewish group attachment such as culture, ingroup marriage, peoplehood, and concern with group interests. The ethnicity of Jews is assessed through an identity that reflects the perceptions of others, a self-conception consisting of the internalized attitudes they hold about themselves, and ingroup associations that give a measure of tangible expression to the patterns of ethnic identity.

The socialization of Los Angeles Jews is very heavily dependent on ingroup processes that link friends and kin together in formal and informal relationships. As neighborhoods change and mobility increases, Jews are finding new ways to maintain historic associations and group distinctiveness. Social relationships are important in identity formation, so that ethnic identity can be measured through formal and informal association with other Jews. The data show that Jews in Los Angeles with a strong Jewish identity are more likely to have other Jews as their best friends, but even those with a weaker Jewish identity have more Jewish than non-Jewish friends.

A number of attitudinal and behavioral indicators are associated with high scores on the national identity (peoplehood) subscale. Persons who do volunteer work in Jewish organizations have a stronger Jewish identity than those who are not active. Higher scores are evident among Jews who are more interested in sending their children to a Jewish summer camp as well as among those whose parental homes were warm and emotionally supportive. This pattern is also in evidence for Los Angeles Jews who were active in Jewish groups as teenagers and whose parents were supportive of Jewish organizations (see Table 37).

A Jewish Sensitivity Index was developed in order to assess differential degrees of response to the public visibility of Jews. The scale measures reactions to the use of the words "Jew" or "Jewish" in mixed company, Jewish visibility in the news, behavior in the company of Gentiles, the wearing of a yarmulke in public, and a stranger assuming the respondent was Jewish. Los Angeles Jews with a strong national identity or sense of Jewish peoplehood are

TABLE 37

CHARACTERISTICS OF THOSE WHO SCORED HIGH ON JEWISH NATIONAL IDENTITY (PEOPLEHOOD) SCALE (%)

			x^2, p. <
	Warm	**Not Warm**	
Environment of parents' home was warm	80.8	70.2	.05
	Active	**Not Active**	
Parents active in or supported Jewish organizations	59.1	44.0	.01
	Yes	**No**	
Active in teen Jewish organizations	64.2	42.0	.001
	Yes	**No**	
Respondent active in or volunteers in Jewish organizations	63.0	48.5	.05
	Yes	**No**	
Plan to send child to Jewish summer camp	65.8	44.0	.001
	High Sensitivity	**Low Sensitivity**	
Jewish sensitivity scale	54.6	38.1	.01

more likely to be sensitive to the ways in which Jews are viewed in the public milieu. This suggests that those Jews who have the most powerful feelings of belonging to their group are also the most concerned about how they are seen by others.

Some in the Jewish community hold the view that young Jews, particularly the grandchildren and great-grandchildren of the immigrants, are secure and comfortable in their Jewishness (Silberman, 1985). This perception is not supported by the data for Los Angeles Jews that indicate an increase over generations in high Jewish sensitivity scores as measured by the Jewish Sensitivity Index. By the fourth generation, 70.7% of Los Angeles Jews have a high degree of Jewish sensitivity and tend to be uncomfortable when Jews or Jewishness become matters of public discussion.

This can be a special problem for large numbers of Jews who conduct their business and professional activities in the non-Jewish world. They tend to live in mixed residential areas, and secular education has taken precedence over Jewish education. As many participate actively in the areas of literature, drama, the arts, and music, their values and commitments move outside the sphere of their Jewish existence. They tend to see their American and Jewish identities as separate, and in most activities they act as Americans and only on particular occasions as Jews. Jewish life occupies limited regions of their life space and is in keeping with the American ideology of strict separation between the religious and secular spheres.

Despite these conscious and unconscious processes, most Jews have developed an attachment to their ethnic group as well as to members of the group who share many characteristics and perspectives. Cultural and other influences add to the personal core of their identity, and psychological patterns emerge that tend to be tribal rather than intellectual or philosophical. Sometimes special language, unique humor, and religious rituals are employed which, when joined with shared values, reinforce this group consciousness and the maintenance of Jewish identity.

What has not been widely understood is that Jews who are part of industrialized or modern society often need their traditional bases in order to express their desires for self-determination. They have a religion and culture with a particular set of values, beliefs, and practices passed down from generation to generation that exercise a powerful influence on behavior. There are congregations, organizations, festivals, and other forms of human association without which the individual would be lost in the vast structures of government, community, and industry.

For Los Angeles Jews, ethnic identity is a social and psychological phenomenon intertwined with other factors such as urbanization and technology that also affect their lives. While the patterns of identification are altered in terms of membership, content, and saliency, these changes do not denigrate their continuing validity for members of the Jewish community. This leads increasingly to a search for Jewish connections and involvements as individuals seek personal meaning that can be a form of tribalism as well as a vehicle for combating alienation and providing purpose and direction in life.

Section 3

From Grandparents to Grandchildren

Introduction to Section 3

The adjustment to America has led to uncertainty and anxiety among all generations of American Jews, from the immigrants determined to survive in a new and sometimes hostile environment to the third and fourth generations seeking clarity about what it means to be Jewish in a plural society. Jews today are a transgenerational group whose most important characteristic is a more or less common culture that manifests aspects of contemporary life as it reaches into an historical past.

None of the generations is homogeneous with some in each generation having acculturated more rapidly than others. This suggests that common experience may be as important as the chronological generation of Jews in assessing group identity and understanding the nature of the Jewish community (Waxman, 1981). But people within different generations tend to have similar outlooks and behavior patterns because of shared experiences and values, and there are markedly discernible patterns of change from generation to generation (Dashefsky and Shapiro,1974).

The search for Jewish identity is a special problem for Jewish youth since there are not too many adults available to help them examine the problem openly and honestly. In the past, Jewish identity developed naturally as young people absorbed the qualities of the Jewish home and communal environment. Today, Jewishness is not a matter of natural inheritance as parents are unsure about what it means to be a Jew in America and often lack confidence in their own knowledge and understanding of their Jewishness. The large majority of Jews want their children to be good Jews but prefer that they be neither more nor less observant.

> Our young people are bewildered, perplexed about the meaning of being human, about the meaning of being a Jew. There is a waiting for meaning, but meaning is kept a well-guarded secret. We have a wonderful generation of young people. They are alert, sensitive, eager for understanding, capable of appreciation. It is we who fail them. Instead of conveying the intellectual splendor and the deep humanity of our heritage, we offer them infantile conceptions, stereotypes, clichés (Heschel, 1965).

Most young Jews have grown up in a culture that is essentially non-Jewish and that makes it difficult for them to accept Jewish values and traditions. There is no personal consistency or coherent set of rules to prepare them for participation in Jewish life, so they often reject the Jewish community and the world of their parents. They are troubled by the fragmentation of contemporary life and the corrupting influences of modern society and immerse themselves in a search for meaningful involvements and experience outside the Jewish sphere. Their skepticism about the systems of meaning that previously guided the lives of Jews motivates them to seek fulfillment in new and non-traditional ways (Sleeper, 1973). Increasing numbers of Jewish youth are involved in cults and other variant behaviors, and this is now a subject of serious discussion within the Jewish community.

There are also signs that suggest the rebellious and searching generation of young Jews is involved in a quest for traditional Jewish values and roots that challenges previous accomodations to secularism and self-gratification. As a result of the search for inner meaning, havurot and other structures are developing based on fellowship, intimacy, and mutual concern. This is reflected for some in a return to communal affiliation, observance of selected Jewish rituals, and limited degrees of synagogue attendance. The resurgence of Jewish interest and commitment is further stimulated by the development of ethnic pride as a legitimate condition of American life that provides psychological support for the individual in a group context. A reacculturation process is taking place that seeks to confront the serious problems of Jewish assimilation and attrition threatening the future of the Jewish community.

The organized American Jewish community of twenty or thirty years ago was led by people who were universalists and integrationists, but it is currently controlled by those who take pride in Jewish communal and political assertiveness. This turning inward of Jewish leadership focuses on specifically Jewish needs and concerns and is accompanied by a diminution of general community activities. One of the reasons for this readjustment is anxiety about assimilative processes that diminish Jewish identity and communal affiliation, so that "Jewish survivalism" has become the principal ideology of Jewish communal life and has taken on the qualities of a civil religion.

While survivalism is sometimes grounded in religious conviction, it is more often a widespread endorsement of civil Jewish values and beliefs expressed through communal involvement. The core of civil Judaism is in its emphasis on the mutual responsibility of Jews, the centrality of Israel which expresses the empowerment of the Jewish people, and the need to challenge both the internal and external threats to Jewish survival through political activities as well as the philanthropic aspects of tzedakah. It emerges through the specific institutional activities of such groups as Jewish federations and the United Jewish Appeal, and an entire generation of Jewish communal leadership has been shaped by its tenets (Woocher, 1980).

Jewish political power developed with great force after the Yom Kippur War when Israelis fought to defend themselves and diaspora Jews rallied around them. Aid for Israel has grown enormously through Jewish efforts here and abroad, and political influence is manifested on behalf of Soviet Jews, allocations for the Jewish poor, and other domestic communal needs. Jewish survivalists are involved in vigorous political activities including Jewish Political Action Committees (PACS) in the belief that Jews can and must shape their own destiny. And many Jews have been elected to the U.S. Congress and Senate in a marked departure from earlier generations that felt Jews would be safer if they maintained a low political profile.

Although American Jews are often isolated, self-centered, and particularistic, they are still more committed to social justice and social welfare changes than members of most groups. Today, however, increasing numbers of Jews are supporting programs labeled as conservative, including opposition to school busing and quotas, promises of lower taxation, tougher law enforcement to contain crime and pornography, and support for the family and the neighborhood. Moreover, many are moving away from their traditional support for civil liberties by rejecting the absolutist concept of free speech for those who espouse Nazi-type views.

But the conservative trend among Jews is not very deep as they continue to be socially concerned in their personal and political orientations. They are still fearful of the new right and the Moral Majority which espouse a Christian vision for America grounded in the imposition of prayer in the schools and support for Christian political candidates. Jews do not support outlawing abortion, repeal of social legislation, and drastic cuts in health and welfare programs.

While there is no longer a total congruence between American liberalism and Jewish political preferences, the Jewish political agenda does not represent a significant swing to the right. The perceived conservatism of Jews may well be a centrism or moderation that accepts the social gains starting with the New Deal, but expresses a sense of caution in the adoption of radical measures to cure our social ills (Jerusalem Institute of Federal Studies, 1981).

The survivalist philosophy has been fueled by ongoing reports of anti-Semitic incidents in the United States and in Western Europe. Vandalism against Jewish property, swastika paintings, and the desecration of cemeteries and institutions have aroused deep concern among Jews. Terrorist attacks against synagogues, restaurants, and other places have created a climate of unease and uncertainty that bring forth memories of the Nazi Holocaust. Efforts by those seeking to convince the world that the Holocaust was a hoax have added to a sense of anxiety and beleaguerment. This concern has been reinforced by the growth of anti-Semitism among American blacks stimulated, in part, by Louis Farrakhan of the Nation of Islam whose views remain largely unrepudiated by black officials.

At the same time, some Jewish leaders caution that anti-Jewish acts are attributable to widespread anti-social behavior and do not represent a massive resurgence of anti-Semitism. This view is given support by findings of polls from the 1960s to the present that point to a sharp decline in prejudice against Jews in America and a significant increase in their social acceptance as individuals and as members of a group. Although Jews are less than 3% of the population and are concentrated in major metropolitan regions, they participate freely in most areas of endeavor and Judaism is perceived as one of the three principal faiths in America (Rosenfield, 1982). Moreover, it is well to remember that anti-Semitism never developed a political base nor has it been institutionalized in this country.

Still, there is increasing public discussion about the "Jewish lobby" and the perception that Israel, working through Jews in this country, has a veto over American foreign policy. Some view the resistance to Jews exercising group pressure as a new form of the old anti-Semitism that is reflected in non-acceptance of the right of Jews as a collective body to seek support for Israel. In the United Nations, it is not the individual Jew who is the target of this new anti-Semitism but, rather, the Jewish national entity, the State of Israel. Consequently, while there is less of the traditional anti-

Semitism as measured by the acceptance of Jews as neighbors, in employment, and education there is an emergence of a political anti-Semitism that seeks to impact on Jewish interests.

While overt anti-Semitism has diminished greatly, the fear persists that nativist movements as well as events pertaining to Israel will stimulate greater anti-Semitism. Indeed, 51% of Americans feel anti-Semitism in the United States is likely to increase because of events in the Middle East, while 77% of American Jews feel this way (*Newsweek,* October 4, 1982). Moreover, 66% of American Jews believe anti-Semitism is a very important issue in this country, and an additional 13% see it as somewhat important (Cohen, 1982).

The impact and memory of the Holocaust give powerful impetus to the survivalist viewpoint and are central to an understanding of Jewish identity today. The Holocaust affects the way Jews perceive themselves and relate to others in the non-Jewish world. There has been a gradual unfolding of comprehension and confrontation with its meaning and how the destruction of the European Jewish community has diminished Jewish life everywhere. The loss of millions of Jews has significantly impacted the shape of the Jewish future by reducing the vitality and strength of the Jewish people, and serves to deepen a sense of Jewish consciousness as well as a reaffirmation of Jewish identity and survival (Herman, 1977).

Study of the Holocaust has become a respected academic specialty with a growing list of publications, over seven hundred courses in institutions of higher learning, courses and units in public school systems, and the preparation of significant curricular material. But some educators and religious leaders fear that focusing on the Holocaust in order to deepen Jewish awareness can be harmful to young people by distorting the spiritual richness and meaning of Jewish life. If it becomes virtually the only aspect of Jewish history studied in Jewish and non-Jewish schools, it may be exaggerated and misinterpreted to imply that Jewish survival depends on external pressures such as anti-Semitism. Moreover, the power of the Holocaust to influence a sense of Jewishness may diminish over time because hostility does not explain the survival of Judaism or satisfy the spiritual and emotional needs of the Jewish people.

Establishment of the State of Israel transformed the Zionist movement into a reality that has had a revolutionary impact on Jews throughout the world. Classical Zionist doctrine was based on the view that Jewish life in the diaspora was unfulfilling and temporary, and that a Jewish homeland would be a place of authentic creativity where Jews would control their own destiny. What has happened, however, is that only 20% of world Jewry live in Israel, while most of those who do not have made it a central tenet of their Jewishness.

Israeli Jews and some in America believe that Jewish life is incomplete outside of Israel. The Jewish community in Israel sees itself as a verification of Zionist ideology and as pointing up the inadequacy of a diaspora solution to the problems of Jewish survival and Judaism. There is the continued belief that life in the diaspora is "exile" and an assertion of the need for an ingathering of Jews to Israel. Most American Jews feel that Israel is central to the Jewish experience, but they also believe that the American diaspora has been vital to Jewish survival because it has contributed to the defeat of Nazism, opened up the Soviet Union for Jewish emigration, and provided essential support for the well-being of the Jewish State. For the most part, Jews in this country are firmly rooted in American culture and believe in the viability of a healthy and creative Jewish life here.

Although fully supportive of Israel's social, economic, and political needs, some American Jews are expressing negative feelings about particular issues affecting relations between the United States and Israel. The increasing strain between the American government and Israel has added to the pressures on American Jewry and is producing internal tensions and conflicts within the American Jewish community. Some of this is related to concern about the ongoing perception that Jews have a dual loyalty to this country and to Israel.

Nonetheless, Israel is a primary cultural and spiritual resource for American Jews, and Jewish education for young people and adults frequently involves study tours and activities in Israel from archeology to sunbathing. There are programs of work and study including service in kibbutzim, learning at Israeli institutions, and various educational and cultural endeavors involving Israel and the United States. Although Israeli institutions are playing some part in the education of American Jews, Israel has the potential for becoming an even greater factor in the processes of American Jewish education. The belief of most Jewish leaders is that deepening the exposure of American and Israeli Jews to one another will lead to a more profound understanding of the validity of their respective experiences.

Israel has become the focus of American Jewry's civil religion, especially for those who have broken with Jewish sacramentalism (Liebman, 1973 and Sklare and Greenblum, 1967). The overwhelming majority have been stirred by Israel's birth and crises and see its survival as a matter of their own self-interest. As American Jews feel increasingly that their fate is linked with that of Israel, the sense of peoplehood that embraces their concern for Jews all over the world has been strengthened. It is Israel that made the global Jewish community resilient enough to rebound from the shock of the Holocaust, and it is the relentless attacks on Israel and Zionism in the international arena that continue to stimulate militant Jewish involvement and support for its existence.

VI

Generations: The Second Law of Return

In the past, Jewishness was absorbed by young people as they grew up in Jewish community and family environments. No parental decision was involved in the creation of a sense of Jewish identification in the young person's growing identity and self-image. They were immersed in a culture where Jewish language, behavior, and symbolism developed as automatic responses to various situations. Today, most Jews have grown up without the support of such a community where Jewishness is not a matter of natural inheritance.

Many Jews in Los Angeles have special problems in dealing with their Jewish identity because of the enormous pressures for conformity from those, including some Jews, who set the cultural and behavioral tone of the larger community. Los Angeles Jews are participating in a multigenerational process of learning new values, lifestyles, and emotional patterns. As Jewish youth try to follow changing American trends and models, they often come into conflict with their own group. This can lead to the psychic repression of their Jewishness which is sometimes reinforced by their families and friends and contributes to a certain amount of alienation.

The problem is often exacerbated when young Los Angeles Jews leave home and interact with new groups of people and intellectual challenges that replace whatever Jewishness was a part of their scale of values. Many are later resocialized into the Jewish community once they marry and have children but there remains a problem for Judaism on the campus. In their response to the Jewish past and the American environment, young people are changing their behavior, beliefs, and self-definition as Americans and as Jews. This is undergirded by a process in which the success and affluence of some Jews contributes to the diminution of their Jewishness and leads to increased acculturation.

The situation was very different for the immigrants who had a clearly defined way of life grounded in a relatively homogeneous culture, and who were largely concerned with economic survival and adjusting to a new environment. Even those who had abandoned many of the mores of the shtetl and adopted Socialist and secular thought had a traditional sense of Jewish identity. Most immigrant Jews in Los Angeles accepted ritual and moral obligations, participated in religious holidays and festivals, and continued more or less regular patterns of worship. But there were different ways of adjusting in all generations, and a significant gap developed between the immigrant generation and their children, as well as between the children and grandchildren.

As indicated in Chapter V, there are differential degrees of Jewish identity in all generations of Los Angeles Jewry. The children of the immigrants had the problem of living in two cultures: in the American environment where they were considered too foreign, and in the homes of their parents where they were seen as too American. For this second generation acculturation proceeded rapidly, largely through the public schools and mass media communication. The traditions of the group lost their hold on individuals as they became Americanized and learned to perceive the culture of their parents as inferior by the standards of the larger culture (Marden and Meyer, 1968 and Warner, 1953). When this was combined with their own lack of acceptance by non-Jews and non-Jewish institutions, a psychological marginality emerged that raised serious problems pertaining to Jewish identity.

It was feared that the rejection of their heritage by second generation Jews would continue into the third and subsequent generations resulting in an ultimate disappearance of the Jewish group and its traditions. Gans (1956) saw a process of social acculturation in his assessment of American Jewry with cohesiveness diminishing as Jews lost their attachment to Judaism and their minority status. Warner (1953) perceived assimilation in terms of the period of time a group had been in America, and Sandberg (1974) defined the consequent decline of ethnicity over generations as "straight-line theory."

While some held the view that ethnicity was diminishing in a more or less straight line, others perceived it as taking new forms. Those who believed there was a reemergence of ethnicity in the third generation felt this group did not feel inferior because the mannerisms and possessions of its members were comparable to those of other citizens. Indeed, a feeling of pride developed among some of them, leading to study of the history and culture of their ancestors. There has been a tendency to view the third generation in terms of what Hansen (1952) described as "the law of return," the resurgence of ethnic identity among young people that followed the decline of ethnicity among their parents. "Hansen's Law" pointed to an anticipated decline of ethnicity in the second generation and a resurgence in the third, with the group gradually thinning out in the fourth and succeeding generations.

> . . . whenever any immigrant group reaches the third-generation stage in its development a spontaneous and almost irresistible impulse arises which forces the thoughts of many people of different professions, different positions in life, and different points of view to interest themselves in that one factor which they have in common: heritage—the heritage of blood (Hansen, 1952).

The renewal of Jewishness among third generation Los Angeles Jews who were largely removed from Yiddish and shtetl culture did not take place as fully as anticipated. They learned their Jewishness from limited exposure to religious schools, as well as from the diluted Jewish backgrounds of family, peers, and community. For the most part they were inadequately equipped to guide their lives Jewishly, with a consequent increase in interdating, intermarriage, and the abandonment of Jewish practices. This was reinforced by a belief in the congruity of values among the major faith groups and the view that Jews were like all other Americans.

It was left to the rise of ethnicity in the 1960s and early 1970s to facilitate a growing awareness and ethnic consciousness among other groups. This was bolstered for Los Angeles Jews and others by a heightened sensitivity to Jewish concerns, as well as a new sense of pride in Jewish achievements in this country and abroad. As ethnicity became increasingly acceptable in American life, Jews of all generations acquired a more open and authentic Jewish identity. What we are witnessing is a differential Jewish renaissance in all generations that can be described as a "second law of return."

This rejuvenation was especially true for the second generation, the children of the immigrants, who had earlier sought to divest themselves of their Jewish characteristics. While this generation proclaimed the idealism of universalism and deprecated the legitimacy of particularlism, it still had an inherited Jewish identity that stemmed from direct exposure to ethnic Jewish experiences and non-acceptance by the Gentile world. As ethnic identity became more and more fashionable, the second generation rejection of ethnicity described by Hansen and others gave way to a resurgence of group awareness and pride greater than that of the third generation. Hansen's Law was superseded by a new generational differentiation and the decline in ethnicity from the first to the third generations could now be accurately defined as "straight-line theory" (see Table 38).

Today there are differing reactions among Jews in Los Angeles who are seeking to find their roots and identity through reestablishing links with various Jewish institutions and Jewish forms of expression. A profound sense of Jewish identity and excitement can be found among many young Los Angeles Jews who are searching for self-understanding and communal identification. These include both affiliated and unaffiliated Jews utilizing traditional and non-traditional approaches, individuals whose Jewish commitment is contributing to a modern Jewish revival.

The changing characteristics of Los Angeles Jews can also be described in socioeconomic terms as they become increasingly well educated, upwardly mobile, and more dispersed in the spreading metropolitan area. Their socioeconomic status has improved markedly from the first to the third generations and has leveled off in the fourth. By the third generation, there was a dramatic shift away from working in family-owned businesses, but a turn around is taking place in the fourth generation with more and more young people working in private businesses owned by their families (see Table 39).

The trend toward higher education has been one of the more remarkable developments of the American Jewish experience. This is reflected in Los Angeles where, from the first to the third generations, the proportion who secured college, graduate, and profes-

TABLE 38

GENERATIONAL CHANGES IN ETHNIC IDENTITY

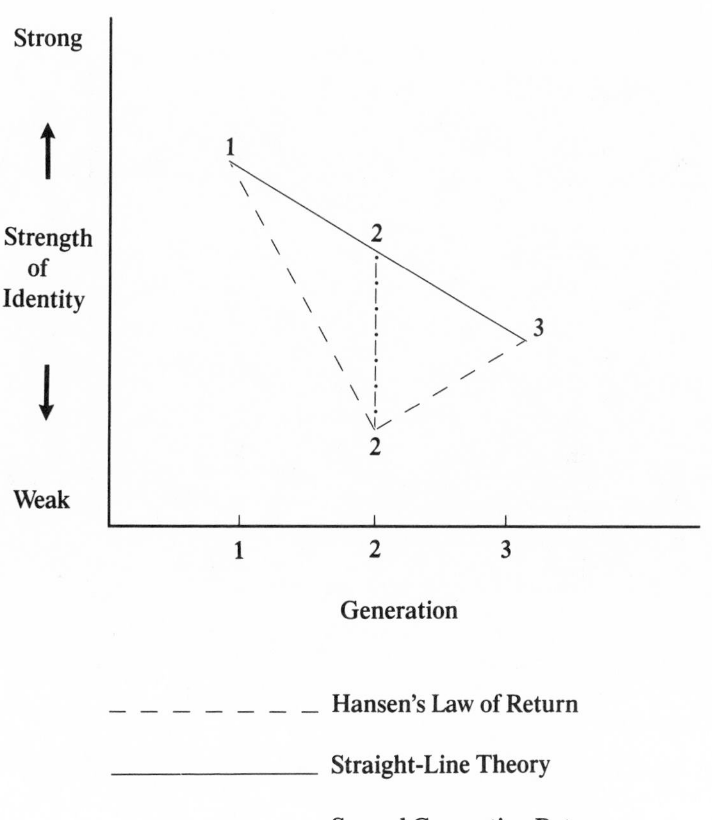

_ _ _ _ _ _ _ Hansen's Law of Return

________________ Straight-Line Theory

_._._._._._._._ Second Generation Return

TABLE 39

HIGH SOCIOECONOMIC STATUS *, COLLEGE EDUCATION, AND FAMILY BUSINESS, BY GENERATION (%)

	Generation				
	1	2	3	4	x^2, p. <
High socioeconomic status	31.6	44.3	65.3	63.5	.001
College graduate or higher	31.2	35.2	54.3	39.0	.01
If in private business, it is family owned	47.3	18.2	19.8	31.3	.01

* High socioeconomic status includes the middle and upper-middle classes.

sional degrees increased to an extraordinary 54.3%. In the fourth generation, however, the figure has declined, to 39.0%. This drop may reflect the fact that some young people have not yet completed their education, but it seems apparent that the move toward higher education among Los Angeles Jews has leveled off from the third to the fourth generations (see Table 39).

Over the years, the residential patterns of Los Angeles Jews have changed as those of the second, third, and fourth generations have moved increasingly to the west side and the San Fernando Valley. The immigrant generation continues to be heavily concentrated in the Jewishly dense urban core with limited movement to other areas. There is a clear trend over the generations toward living in less Jewishly dense areas while, at the same time, Los Angeles Jews express a sense of nostalgia for the warmth and satisfaction of living in a Jewish neighborhood. This contradiction between attitudes and behavior is being resolved by some young Jews who are starting a return to more heavily Jewish environments.

Relationships with family and friends continue to be very important for the Jews of Los Angeles, although some erosion is taking place over time. Second and third generation Jews are the most likely to see their relatives very often, and the first and second generations tend to have more Jewish best friends. The proportion of those who have Jewish best friends declines across the generations, although fourth generation Jews still have more Jewish than non-Jewish friends (see Table 40).

While closeness to family and friends are among the best measures of Jewish kinship, other indicators also shed light on the question of Jewish peoplehood. Items from the Jewish identity scale underscore the ongoing commitment of Los Angeles Jews to other Jews here and abroad. A very high proportion of all Jews say they feel obliged to help world Jewry, with an upturn evident in the fourth generation. However, this is not as yet reflected in giving patterns to Jewish causes, and the second generation is far more charitable than any of the others. There is also a very strong belief, including the fourth generation, that "you can be for your own people first and still be a good American" (see Table 41).

Intermarriage in Los Angeles is increasing at an extraordinary rate as the behavior of Jews closely follows their changing attitudes toward such marriages as well as to the practice of interdating (see Chapter II). Although there were some intermarriages in the first

TABLE 40

SEE RELATIVES OFTEN, HAVE JEWISH BEST FRIENDS, BY GENERATION (%)

	Generation				
	1	2	3	4	x^2, p. <
Sees relatives very often	64.4	74.7	74.5	63.2	.05
Best friend no. 1 is Jewish	86.4	81.6	66.4	60.3	.001
Best friend no. 2 is Jewish	82.5	82.8	65.6	56.5	.001

TABLE 41

STATISTICALLY SIGNIFICANT ITEMS FROM THE JEWISH IDENTITY SCALE, BY GENERATION (%)

	Generation				
	1	2	3	4	x^2, p. <
Too bad more young people not continuing Jewish tradition	91.4	90.0	71.2	74.6	.001
Jews should read Jewish books, periodicals	81.9	75.6	59.7	66.1	.01
I like to listen to Jewish music	92.7	75.6	59.3	62.1	.001
Jewish education essential for Jewish survival	97.6	87.8	84.3	77.6	.01
Important to learn Hebrew	40.2	41.1	41.7	61.0	.05
Better to marry a Jew	81.7	77.5	65.6	49.2	.001
Feel obliged to help world Jewry	90.2	89.8	70.1	74.1	.001
Can be for your own people first and still be a good American	90.2	86.4	75.4	84.7	.05
Important encourage Jewish identification in children	93.9	100.0	84.9	86.4	.001
Important for me to contribute time, resources to temple	53.7	50.6	34.6	37.3	.05
Enjoy religious services to be with other Jews	67.1	53.9	41.7	41.4	.01
I enjoy participating in synagogue programs	57.3	48.3	40.9	36.2	.05
Pesach Seders important to me	82.9	74.2	63.8	63.8	.05
Jewish prayers help me when I am troubled	52.4	37.1	28.6	26.3	.01

and second generations, the upturn in later generations has been very evident. The data in Table 42 show that 28.8% of the third and 43.5% of the fourth generations are married to non-Jews. There is also a straight line decrease across generations of those who believe it is better to marry a Jew, with changing attitudes toward endogamous marriage heralding such behavior (see Table 41).

Social interaction with non-Jews of the opposite sex starts early and is growing among Los Angeles Jews. The proportion of those who always dated Jews in their teen years and later declines sharply over the generations, so that by the fourth generation interdating is the overwhelming practice. As dating non-Jews becomes the norm for Jews in their teen years, it accelerates when they move into adulthood (see Table 42). Moreover, the desire of parents to restrict interdating also declines by generation in a more or less straight line. Personal contact across group lines is a reinforcing element of this process as Jews of the second, third, and fourth generations are more likely to be active in non-Jewish than in Jewish organizations, especially in their teen years.

As indicated in Chapter III, the combined rate of congregational and Jewish communal affiliation in Los Angeles is relatively low. Analysis by generation shows that membership in either a religious or Jewish communal institution or both declines from the second to the third generations and turns up in the fourth generation. Moreover, there is a decline by generation of Los Angeles Jews who feel that synagogue membership is too expensive (see Table 43).

It is in the area of affiliation with Jewish communal organizations that the fourth generation upturn occurs at a more powerful level of significance. At the same time, there is a sharp decline from the third to the fourth generations in non-Jewish organizational membership. The data point to a first generation that is much more likely to belong to Jewish organizations, and a second generation moving strongly into non-Jewish groups while holding on to their Jewish affiliations. In the third generation, affiliation with Jewish organizations declines dramatically, while non-Jewish organizational affiliations remain constant (see Table 43). Among those who are religiously affiliated, the trend by generations shows a fourth generation increase among Orthodox and Reform Jews and a decline among Conservative Jews (see Table 44).

However, the religious orientation of all Los Angeles Jews including the unaffiliated indicates a very different set of patterns.

TABLE 42

INTERMARRIAGE AND ALWAYS DATING JEWS, BY GENERATION (%)

	Generation				
	1	2	3	4	x^2, p. <
Have non-Jewish spouse	11.6	12.7	28.8	43.5	.01
Always dated Jews as teenager	64.3	55.7	40.0	18.8	.001
Always dated Jews later	52.9	41.4	22.8	9.8	.001

TABLE 43

BELONG TO JEWISH AND NON-JEWISH GROUPS, BY GENERATION (%)

	Generation				
	1	2	3	4	x^2, p. <
Belong to one or more Jewish organizations	42.9	40.7	16.4	21.9	.001
Belong to one or more congregations	34.5	34.1	24.6	28.1	n.s.
Belong to non-Jewish organizations	20.2	45.1	44.8	30.2	.001
Synagogue membership too expensive	66.7	62.6	54.5	37.5	.01

TABLE 44

SYNAGOGUE WITH WHICH RESPONDENTS ARE AFFILIATED, BY GENERATION

	Generation			
	1	2	3	4
Orthodox	28.9	32.4	4.4	9.0
Conservative	55.3	43.2	53.3	32.0
Reform	15.8	24.4	42.3	59.0
	100.0%	100.0%	100.0%	100.0%

x^2, $p. < .01$

There are many who consider themselves Orthodox Jews even while not belonging to congregations. The trend for those who call themselves Conservative Jews shows a strong fourth generation upturn, suggesting that many of the younger unaffiliated appear to be leaning toward this form of traditional Judaism. And while fourth generation affiliated Jews are more likely to be Reform (see Table 44), this generation manifests a sharp decline in Reform orientation after major gains in the third (see Table 45).

The discussion in Chapter III also points to a general decline in patterns of religious observance among Los Angeles Jews. When the data are differentiated by generation, the reduction in traditional behaviors is generally apparent from the first to the third generations, with a leveling off or upturn of interest in the fourth generation. These changes have been influenced, to some extent, by the religious observance of the respondents' parents as well as by the degree to which parents joined with their children in Sabbath services. Jewish youth look to their parents as religious models and prefer them as companions at religious services (Jewish Welfare Federation of New Orleans, 1966 and Sklare and Greenblum, 1967).

There is a decline from the first to the third generations among those who always or usually light Sabbath candles, buy kosher meat, use separate dishes, and attend Sabbath services. But there is a substantial increase in buying kosher meat among fourth generation Jews, with lesser gains shown in using separate dishes, lighting Sabbath candles, and attending Sabbath services. As for the religious behavior of the parents of respondents, there is a straight line decline by generations in perceptions of coming from a religious home. Nonetheless a higher proportion of fourth generation Jews report that their fathers and mothers attended services with them, which may be one of the more significant elements in the analysis of the fourth generation "return" to Jewishness (see Table 46).

A further dimension of the renewal of Jewish interest among fourth generation Los Angeles Jews pertains to the tremendous change in attitudes toward having children. The demographic patterns for Jews in recent years have underscored a continuing decline in the number of children in Jewish families. In the fourth generation, however, Los Angeles Jews are twice as likely as the third generation to view having three or more children as ideal for a Jewish couple (see Table 47). If this perception is acted out in the

TABLE 45

RESPONDENT'S CURRENT RELIGIOUS ORIENTATION, BY GENERATION

	Generation			
	1	2	3	4
Orthodox	50.0	45.6	26.2	27.0
Conservative	21.4	35.6	31.3	42.8
Reform	28.6	18.8	42.5	30.2
	100.0%	100.0%	100.0%	100.0%

x^2, p. $<$ .001

TABLE 46

PARENT'S OBSERVANCE, BY RESPONDENT'S GENERATION (%)

	Generation				
	1	2	3	4	x^2, p. <
Lights Sabbath candles	33.3	19.8	11.9	12.5	.001
Buys kosher meat	22.6	9.9	6.7	14.1	.05
Uses separate dishes	17.9	5.6	3.7	4.7	.05
Attends Sabbath services	20.4	12.0	7.4	9.8	.10
Parent's home was religously observant	67.5	50.5	30.3	25.0	.001
Father attended services with me	51.2	30.7	10.7	19.0	.001
Mother attended services with me	43.9	25.3	12.9	17.4	.001

TABLE 47

IDEAL NUMBER OF CHILDREN FOR A JEWISH FAMILY, BY GENERATION

Ideal Number of Children	Generation			
	1	2	3	4
0 - 2	41.7	52.7	66.4	57.8
3 - 6	41.7	23.1	14.2	28.1
No opinion	16.6	24.2	19.4	14.1
	100.0%	100.0%	100.0%	100.0%

x^2, p. < .001

fourth and later generations, the increase in the number of Jews in the population could have a positive and far-reaching impact on the future of Jewish life.

As indicated in Chapter III, the sense of peoplehood among Los Angeles Jews is focused, to a considerable degree, on support for the State of Israel and a commitment to its security and well-being. Although 70% have never been to Israel and only one-fourth are planning to visit there soon, the Jewish State is seen as a great source of strength and pride in all generations. Membership in Zionist groups has declined sharply from the first to the fourth generations, and it is clear that very few Jews are considering aliyah, emigration to Israel. Nonetheless, there is a growing desire among Los Angeles Jews to send their children to programs in Israel, with a straight line increase culminating in 39.1% of the fourth generation holding this view (see Table 48).

While most Jewish families claim to place a high value on Jewish education for their children, a considerable proportion of Los Angeles Jews have received little or none. There is a decline by generation of those who have received a "heavy" Jewish education, while the number of Los Angeles Jews who have had a "moderate" Jewish education has increased. The proportion of those who had "little or no" Jewish education is greatest in the second generation, even though this generation believes strongly that it is essential for Jewish survival. A lack of Jewish education may have contributed to the processes of acculturation and assimilation that impacted this generation before the upsurge of ethnic awareness and pride stimulated many to return to Jewishness (see Tables 41 and 49).

As noted in Chapter IV, the percentage of Los Angeles Jews who understand Yiddish and Hebrew well has declined over time, so that by the fourth generation only 1.6% understand Yiddish and 4.7% have a good knowledge of Hebrew. This latter figure contrasts sharply with the upturn to 61.0% of fourth generation Jews who feel it is important to learn Hebrew. The gap is offset in part by the additional 31.3% who claim to have at least a little knowledge of the language. There are other hopeful signs of renewed Jewish cultural interest in the fourth generation including support for Jewish music and reading and the need for young people to carry on the Jewish tradition (see Table 41).

As for the Jewish reading habits of Los Angeles Jews, there is considerable involvement across generations in reading books on

TABLE 48

VIEWS ABOUT ISRAEL AND ZIONISM, BY GENERATION (%)

	Generation				
	1	2	3	4	x^2, p. <
Israel a source of strength and pride	88.9	90.0	74.6	76.2	.01
Israel a place for Jews to decide own destiny	80.0	69.7	57.0	67.2	.01
Has visited Israel one or more times	47.6	28.9	26.8	15.6	.01
Plans to visit Israel next year or so	30.5	41.1	17.3	20.6	.01
Ever been a Zionist	30.1	24.4	13.6	1.6	.001
Plans to send children to programs in Israel	15.9	24.1	31.9	39.1	.05

Jewish topics, but a decline is evidenced from the second to the fourth generations in reading local Jewish newspapers and Jewish magazines. The drop in readership tends to level off from the third to the fourth generations which points to some holding on of interest regarding Jewish news and issues.

TABLE 49

JEWISH EDUCATION, BY GENERATION

	Generation			
	1	2	3	4
Little or none	30.4	50.6	44.4	42.8
Moderate	55.1	42.0	50.8	54.0
Heavy	14.5	7.4	4.8	3.2
	100.0%	100.0%	100.0%	100.0%

x^2, p. < .05

What is apparent among Los Angeles Jews is an increase over the generations of interdating and intermarriage, together with a decline in affiliation, observance, Jewish education, and some Jewish reading habits. There is continuing concern about anti-Jewish discrimination and extremism of the right and the left, as well as a sensitivity to public manifestations of Jewishness. At the same time, there has been a noticeable and encouraging upturn of Jewish interest among many fourth generation Jews, with increasing rates of religious and communal affiliation, ongoing support for Israel, and even a desire to reverse the downturn in Jewish births by having more children.

Young Jews in Los Angeles are still largely outside the framework of organized Jewish life despite the desire of many to find appropriate ways of expressing their Jewishness. The neglect of the singles group by Jewish institutions is underscored by their under-representation on Federation, synagogue, and agency boards. Fortunately, some changes are taking place in the attitudes and practices of Jewish leadership as witnessed by new outreach programs directed toward the young. If there is to be a vital and creative Jewish community, this area of need deserves greater recognition and investment of Jewish resources. There is a significant reanimation of Jewish interest into the fourth generation that remains to be tapped and that can materially benefit the Jewish community of the future.

VII

Survivalism: The New Jews, Los Angeles Style

Los Angeles Jews have been torn between the compelling values of Jewish group survival and the pull toward integration into the formal and informal structures of society. The Jewish and social concerns of Los Angeles Jewry cover a broad spectrum ranging from a total commitment to Jewish interests here and abroad to an exclusive communal orientation in the non-Jewish civic milieu. A very large segment of the Jewish population is involved in both Jewish and societal concerns, while others are active in neither. Jews have an abiding commitment to the security and health of Israel as well as a deep concern with ongoing manifestations of anti-Semitism. They are politically aware and active on behalf of Jewish interests here and abroad, while they continue to feel socially responsible for the well-being of all. In effect, the Jews of Los Angeles are widely differentiated in terms of their Jewish and community obligations and activities.

In recent years, there has been a growth of Jewish political expression stemming from a recognition of distinct group needs that have a political dimension. Jews recall with anguish their passivity of many centuries that culminated in the slaughter of six million in the Holocaust. A desire to control their own destiny has influenced the vigorous political activity of Jewish "survivalists" who are determined that never again will Jews be defenseless victims of political terror. The mindset of Jews changed radically as Jews in Israel fought to defend themselves and diaspora Jews rallied around them. Jewish political power was maximized on behalf of Soviet Jewry through the Jackson-Vanik Amendment, and aid for Israel grew significantly through American and worldwide efforts to shape a Jewish future (Greenberg, 1981).

Today, Jewish political activity contributes to Jewish identity by mobilizing individual and group support for Israel, Soviet Jewry, and other Jewish needs. Emotions are often raised to a fever pitch regarding such issues as the sale of planes and arms to Saudi Arabia, with these conflicts providing a vehicle for galvanizing American Jews into expressing themselves politically and, thereby, reinforcing their Jewish identity. Jewish groups are also asserting themselves by seeking a share of government allocations and by providing inputs into public policy-making that affects such allocations. Many of these activities are concerned with the Jewish poor and other domestic Jewish communal needs that are distinct from pro-Israel lobbying.

What is emerging among Los Angeles Jews and others is the concept of "survivalism" whose core is a "civil Jewish faith" committed to the perpetuity of the Jewish group, not only in its spiritual dimensions, but through political organization and involvement directed toward protecting Jewish interests. This has been accompanied by a strong rise in the ethnic-cultural dimensions of Jewish identity, as well as the overarching presence, inspiration, and claims of the State of Israel. Fulfillment of the Jewish mission for Los Angeles Jews is most often exemplified by responses to the question: "Is it good or bad for the Jews?"

Los Angeles Jews who are the most dedicated to dealing with these issues tend to be the members and leaders of over five hundred organizations affiliated with the Jewish Federation Council, as well as those identified with the many temples and synagogues throughout the metropolitan area. Still, others not involved in Jewish organizations favor using political influence almost as often as those at the highest levels of involvement. For most in the leadership echelons and many in the rank and file, survivalism is the ideology of the future and a strongly Jewish definition has emerged of their accepted responsibilities. There is a focus not only on the physical survival of Jews, but on the survival of Jewish culture and tradition, including education and religion. Survivalist policies govern the programs of most Jewish institutions in a framework of commitment to the perpetuation of the Jewish people.

Concern with Israel's future has become a major focus of the activities of individuals and organizations in the Los Angeles Jewish community. Zionist groups continue to function in the Los Angeles diaspora even though their members choose not to move to Israel. Their ideas converge on the unity of the Jewish people and the belief that Jews are linked not only to those who live in the same community but to Jews everywhere. Today, there do not appear to be major pragmatic distinctions between Zionists and non-Zionists, for the test of Zionist commitment that calls for settlement in Israel is not being met by either group.

Since the creation of Israel, there has been a resurgence of interest in Jewish life in Los Angeles and the strengthening of an all-embracing sense of Jewish peoplehood. The Jewish community is working toward the survival of Judaism in a culturally and politically plural society under conditions of freedom. At the same time, there is a sense of urgency to support Israel because of its vulnerability to threats from the Arab nations and their allies throughout the world. Aggressive self-defense has substituted for the previous passivity and acquiescence of Jews everywhere. Los Angeles Jews identify with the Israelis who defend themselves and their country with courage and sacrifice and give material support to this identification by their financial contributions and by visiting Israel.

There are networks of association between the Israeli and Los Angeles Jewish communities in social, economic, religious, and cultural areas. However, in periods of crisis, the focus is on the political aspects of that relationship—the policies of the American and Israeli governments in relation to the physical security of Israel and the survival of its people. It also relates to economic and military aid from the United States to Israel that stems from a self-conscious determination by Jews as an ethnic-religious community to participate in the development and survival of Israel. This activity is stimulated by the shared values and moral principles that govern relationships between the two countries, and is based on the recognition that Israel is a democratic society. Moreover, it is grounded in the American national interest since Israel serves as a barrier to further Soviet penetration of the Middle East (American Jewish Committee, 1978).

The data show that more than 80% of Los Angeles Jews believe it is important to try to influence American policy on behalf of Israel. Both the affiliated and unaffiliated, those with stronger and weaker Jewish identities, and people of all ages and socioeconomic backgrounds share this view to a substantial degree. Even in the event of a policy conflict between America and Israel, Los Angeles Jews divide down the middle in terms of where to place their support. While this might be seen as an expression of dual loyalty, the reality is that most Jews see a commonality between the interests of Israel and the United States so that their American patriotism is not diminished by this challenge.

Perpetuation of the memory of the Holocaust is now a central part of the civil religion of the Los Angeles Jewish community, acting both as a psychic catharsis and as a communal glue. Holocaust programs are able to connect with virtually all Jews including the secular, disaffected, and even unaffilated. Consciousness of the Holocaust developed slowly after World War II, but by the 1960s it had become a major force in Los Angeles Jewish life. Some of this reaction stemmed from the sense of isolation Jews felt prior to the Six-Day War as well as from the powerful feelings of guilt associated with the plight of Soviet Jewry. Jews sought to remember those who perished and to impress on the minds of non-Jews the historical lessons of indifference that can contribute to group hatred and genocide.

It is no surprise, therefore, that Los Angeles Jews established a number of institutions to study and teach about the Holocaust, as well as organizations of survivors and their children. All of these institutions and others are dedicated to an emphasis on the Holocaust as a predominately Jewish tragedy while understanding its universalistic implications. This consciousness was deepened by the Six-Day War and the Yom Kippur War when another Holocaust was viewed as a distinct possibility. Programs of Jewish and public education are emerging in Jewish, Christian, and public schools in order to strengthen awareness of what transpired during the Holocaust as a means of assuring that such monstrous behavior will never happen again.

Los Angeles Jews are deeply troubled by such groups as the Institute for Historical Review and Truth Missions that seek to denigrate the meaning of the Holocaust by denying its tragic realities. The responses are anxious and shrill as Jews challenge those who deny an event of such catastrophic importance that resulted in the genocidal murder of one-third of the Jewish people. Virtually every

Jew is outraged by the efforts of these self-styled "scholars" and hate groups, and reactions range from lawsuits, to public denunciations, to quiet pain.

Respondents to this study were asked what Jewish children should be taught about the Holocaust—the murder of six million Jews by the Nazis. It seems clear that Los Angeles Jews do not want to forget the Holocaust; indeed, they want their children to be taught everything about it including the savagery of what transpired and the meaning of its inhumanity for all people. There is an underlying belief that an historical awareness is needed in order to assure that what the Jewish people have gone through will not be repeated. Many emphasized the importance of Jews standing up for their rights, for they fear it could happen again. As one respondent said, "Stamp it out as soon as it starts."

Others are concerned about efforts to use the Holocaust as a means of achieving communal cohesion and suggest a balanced approach that recognizes the importance of Holocaust study when it is necessary and appropriate (Lipstadt, 1981). There is also a sense of anxiety regarding the impact of the Holocaust on the minds of small children (Schulweis, 1976), and some rabbis and psychologists suggest teaching about it when they are young adults. But all Jews agree that the Holocaust was one of the worst disasters of world history, that the world will never be the same, and that all people have an obligation to prevent its reoccurence.

The atrocities of the Nazis created an atmosphere after World War II in which anti-Semitism was muted and expressions of concern for the victims prevailed. Feelings of compassion as well as guilt contributed materially to the partition of Palestine and the establishment of a Jewish State. But the climate of understanding and support for Jews in Israel and elsewhere is changing as negative and hostile stereotypes about Jews and Judaism persist, particularly the charges of dual loyalty, unscrupulousness, and aggressiveness. The perception of Jews is also affected by religious teachings which stress that Jews are different from other human beings and that their status in the divine scheme of things marks them as members of a pariah group.

These beliefs are actualized at times in various behavioral forms including social discrimination and exclusion from the executive suites of some major corporations and banks. It is part of an intellectual tradition in which ideas, theories, and symbols are continually reworked and reapplied so that anti-Semitism takes on social, political, economic, theological, and sometimes racial forms.

Jews tend to believe that anti-Semitism is associated with other forms of intolerance and hatred that can pose a threat to democratic life and institutions, and they act to defend the freedoms they enjoy along with the rights and liberties of others. This strategy has been very successful for Jews who have, by and large, prospered and thrived in this country. They are less and less excluded from political, economic, and cultural life, and despite their anxiety about anti-Semitism, they feel that America has provided them with more security and liberty than they have ever known before in their diaspora experience.

Large numbers of Jews in Los Angeles and across the country have gained important places in the artistic, intellectual, political, and academic worlds—as well as in business and the professions. Recent studies suggest there is an overall decline of domestic anti-Semitism, with fewer than one-third of non-Jews willing to accept some negative anti-Semitic stereotypes (Schneider, 1978). A 1981 Yankelovich study indicates that only one out of five white Americans can be characterized as high or moderate in anti-Jewish beliefs (Rosenfield, 1982). And recent Anti-Defamation League reports (1983 and 1984) point to a decline or leveling off in reported anti-Semitic incidents.

Further reinforcement comes from a national poll conducted by the Yankelovich organization in December 1979 that indicates Jews are at the bottom of a list of groups believed to be too powerful. A Gallup Poll commissioned by the American Jewish Committee confirms these findings and shows that Jews are more accepted in the United States, with the percentage of those who hold highly favorable opinions of Jews up in the past six years from 33% to 40%, and those with highly unfavorable opinions down from 4% to 2%. Moreover, the percentage of non-Jewish Americans who approve of marriage between Jews and non-Jews has increased from 59% to 69% (*Jewish Post and Opinion,* April 24, 1981).

Despite these changes, more than 70% of Los Angeles Jews report having experienced anti-Semitism at some time in their lives. Those who are better educated have felt anti-Semitism more than others, probably because they tend to be mobile and have had the most contact with non-Jews. Although they have also encountered considerable anti-Semitism, persons under thirty years of age have had less exposure to it than those who are older.

When asked where a lot or some discrimination and prejudice are experienced by Jews today, the respondents point to exclusion from private clubs as the area of greatest sensitivity, followed by employment, housing, and education (see Table 50). Young, educated Jewish men, especially in the fourth generation, are the most likely to feel there is discrimination against Jews in private clubs and employment, while young people generally perceive somewhat

TABLE 50

PERCEPTIONS OF ANTI-JEWISH PREJUDICE

	Percentage Who Perceive a Lot or Some Anti-Jewish Prejudice and Discrimination
Private clubs	79.1
Employment	62.7
Housing	37.7
Education	37.0

less discrimination in education and housing.

The activities of anti-Jewish individuals, organizations, and even nations has had a substantial impact on the fears of Los Angeles Jewry. The data show that 70.1% believe there is a lot or some danger to Jews from right-wing groups and 56.9% perceive the danger from the left. Individuals of all generations see the threat from the right as greater than that from the left but, by the fourth generation, they are seen as more or less equally dangerous (see Table 51). Concern with both left and right wing organizations is felt mostly by persons fifty years of age or older, but a high percentage of younger people are also very anxious.

Support for civil and religious rights and the free expression of ideas, no matter how objectionable, has been a long standing tenet of Jewish belief. But the view that anti-Semitism is a continuing threat has contributed to a considerable shift in the attitudes of Jews toward free speech. When asked if Nazi-type groups should be prohibited from expressing their anti-Semitic ideas freely, 55.2% of Los Angeles Jews agree. Those with the strongest Jewish identity and Jewish education, the less educated, older people and women are the most willing to deny such expression, while young, educated men tend to be the most free speech oriented. However, there is a surprising upturn of interest in prohibiting these views among young Jews of the fourth generation (see Table 51).

Los Angeles Jews are profoundly concerned with their own group interests and are very anxious to express their ideas in the political and community spheres. In their commitment to protecting Jewish rights everywhere, they are carrying out their group responsibilities in various public ways. When asked what they would be likely to do if they felt strongly about an issue, almost 90% chose voting for a candidate who would support their position. Approximately half would write a letter to a newspaper or to an elected official and one-third would form a group to meet with government representatives. Fewer than 5% say they would do nothing to respond to an important issue, a fact that underscores the public-regardingness of the Los Angeles Jewish community.

What is of special interest is the willingness of Jews to participate in a demonstration, with almost half choosing this form of public action. Those in the middle income category and young people are the most likely to demonstrate, but this kind of response declines with age (see Table 52). The combined use of traditional and non-traditional protest methods points up the new mood of activism so prevalent in Jewish life today.

The philosophy of survivalism has been profoundly affected by the dramatic change in Jewish self-definition with 57.9% of Los Angeles Jews choosing ethnic-cultural as the characteristic best describing Jews, 13.1% selecting nationality, and only 17.2% choosing religion. A generation ago studies revealed that most Jews considered themselves Jewish by virtue of their religious identification with Judaism (Sklare, Vosk, and Zboroski, 1955). The percentage who describe Jews primarily in religious terms goes up together with the rise in family income, so that those who earn $40,000 a year or more are the most likely to see themselves as members of a religious group. Los Angeles Jews who earn the least

TABLE 51

DANGER FROM EXTREMIST GROUPS AND PROHIBITING FREE SPEECH FOR NAZI-TYPE GROUPS, BY GENERATION (%)

	Generation				
	1	2	3	4	x^2, p. <
There is danger to Jews from right-wing groups.	72.3	82.2	67.2	60.9	.05
There is danger to Jews from left-wing groups.	56.6	71.1	50.7	54.7	.05
Prohibit Nazi-type groups from expressing anti-Semitic views	73.8	65.9	39.8	45.9	.001

TABLE 52

WILLINGNESS TO PARTICIPATE IN A PROTEST DEMONSTRATION, BY AGE AND ANNUAL FAMILY INCOME

	Percentage by Age and Income			
	Under 30	30-49	50 and Over	x^2, p. <
Age	66.7	57.3	33.8	.001
	Under $15,000	$15,000 to 39,000	$40,000 and Over	
Income	44.4	59.5	50.7	.05

are more likely to see themselves as a nationality but virtually no one believes that Jews are a racial group.

Perhaps the most interesting analysis comes from an assessment of Jewish self-perceptions according to age. Young Los Angeles Jews, those under thirty, have the strongest disposition of any age category to characterize themselves as members of a religious group. Those who are fifty years of age or older are the most likely to see being Jewish as a nationality and the least likely to perceive Jewishness as ethnic-cultural. It should be remembered, however, that a majority of all age, income, and generational subgroups select the ethnic-cultural option (see Table 53).

TABLE 53

CHARACTERISTICS THAT BEST DESCRIBE JEWS, BY AGE

	Age		
	Under 30	30-49	50 and over
Nationality	7.1	8.5	23.7
Religious	23.5	18.1	14.4
Ethnic-Cultural	63.3	64.9	54.0
All others	6.1	8.5	7.9
	100.0%	100.0%	100.0%

x^2, p. < .01

The extraordinary sensitivity of Jews regarding the possibility of becoming victims of bigotry has led to reasoned policies to promote equal rights and respect for cultural diversity. By and large, Jews continue to believe that a balanced expression of liberalism is the philosophy most conducive to the survival of Jews as a group. Their voting patterns reflect a concern for the poor and support for the welfare state that is matched by their dedication to civil liberties, social welfare, and broadly liberal programs (Clymer, 1978, Fisher, 1979 and M. Himmelfarb, 1973). Many join together in national "defense" organizations that combat prejudice and discrimination against Jews and others, while confronting efforts to foster Christian religious indoctrination. This is part of the American Jewish subculture that values learning, charity, and responsibility for the welfare of others, but it also stems from the concern that a non-just society will adversely affect the security and well-being of Jews.

Liberalism is deeply rooted in the Jewish tradition and embraces the broad framework of universalism that emerged from the Emancipation. Jewish freedom is associated with a liberalism that involves a high regard for the individual and for those who seek to maximize human liberty for all. This was a contributing cause to the fact that some turned to revolutionary and human rights movements in the hope of gaining an acceptance they had been denied. Jews were heavily involved in the Russian Revolution of 1917, the Socialist struggles in Europe and America, widespread human rights activities, opposition to the Vietnam war, and efforts to protect the civil rights of blacks, Chicanos, women, homosexuals, and others.

The liberal movement for racial equality in the middle part of this century sought to overcome prejudice and discrimination by activating the consciousness of Jews and other white Americans to carry out the creed of democracy and egalitarianism. This was done through litigation in the courts and the fight for legislation to legally eliminate discrimination in employment and housing, guarantee voting rights, and deal with poverty and urban blight. The goals were equal treatment by the law, integration, and the use of government assistance to overcome past discrimination.

Many Jews in Los Angeles sought integration into community life as individuals rather than as members of an organized community. While most hoped to survive as Jews, they wanted to be accepted and treated like anyone else in the belief that their Jewishness was irrelevant. With a high level of commitment to the democratic political process Jews became deeply involved in political activities, and liberalism was the expression of Jewish culture for those who were otherwise uninvolved Jewishly. Jewish identity was redefined in terms of leading a moral and ethical life as Jews sought to overcome the impact of religious prejudice and ethnic zealotry (Blau, 1976).

There are a number of Los Angeles Jews who continue to be prominent in the leadership of liberal political movements and who feel they have little or no place in the organized Jewish community. Many unaffiliated Jews are much involved in issues pertaining to social justice, economic welfare, civil liberties, and human rights. Some are searching for a universalist ethic that eliminates group differences in the public sphere while allowing them to retain their nominal identification as Jews. Others have a more specific Jewish orientation for their "progressive" views and seek to mobilize Jewish social and political action. Young Jews identified with the "new politics" are alienated from existing Jewish organizations, viewing them as too narrow and conservative and less sensitive to human rights concerns here and abroad. They are forming new groups to serve as a haven for the unaffiliated and others who feel estranged from the organized Jewish community.

But the political identification of many Jews in Los Angeles has shifted substantially from the liberal and left-wing activism of the first half of the century to a current liberal-moderate orientation that expresses itself in a concern for social change without civic disruption. While most Los Angeles Jews grew up in politically aware and concerned homes, fewer than 15% of their parents are described as supportive of Socialist or left-wing movements. Nostalgia for an immigrant generation that came to this country with egalitarian views rooted in Socialism is a thing of the past. Only 5% of the respondents see themselves as radical, while 41% choose liberal, 35% moderate, and 16% conservative. Along with Jews across the country, their choice of political party continues to be heavily Democrat, although fully one-fourth express no party preference at all.

Los Angeles Jews are very civic minded and just as many give to non-Jewish causes as to those that are Jewish. They overwhelmingly endorse the rights of all Americans to a minimum income and full equality and continue to believe that Jews should support working people in their efforts to form unions. There is also the view that Jews should be concerned with world hunger and work to stop racial discrimination (see Table 54), while supporting organizations and political candidates dedicated to human rights, the needs of the disadvantaged, oppressed minorities, and victims of persecution.

TABLE 54

SOCIAL CONCERN SCALE

	Percentage of Agreement
Every American is entitled to a minimum income	79.9
Hunger and famine are of concern to me	91.6
It is necessary to work for full equality for all people	86.5
Jews should work to stop racial discrimination	88.4
Jews should support working people in their efforts to form unions	62.2

Indeed, the social concern of Jews is clearly associated with Jewish identity as those who are the most Jewish have the strongest sense of human compassion.

School desegregation has been seen as an important litmus test of social concern, and Jews measure up to their liberal reputation in substantial numbers. Almost 60% of Los Angeles Jews agree that school desegregation is an important goal for the country, with approximately one-fourth in disagreement. Younger people are the most supportive of this view, as are those who have at least a college degree.

Beyond the abstraction of desegregation as an intellectual concept is the hard reality of busing as a tangible means for achieving this end. Here, Los Angeles Jews distinguish between busing minority children into their neighborhoods and transporting their own children out. The data indicate that 69.0% of Los Angeles Jewry approve having minority children brought into their neighborhood schools, while 13.3% express a negative view. When it comes to busing their own children, however, only 29.3% are in favor with 48.9% opposed. Once again the better educated are the most willing to be supportive, with women, older people, and the less-educated in opposition. Young Jews of the fourth generation are the least interested in busing their own children which suggests either that they are less liberal or that they have a greater personal stake in the issue.

Almost two-thirds of the Jews in Los Angeles support affirmative action programs that secure jobs and educational opportunities for minorities, with fewer than 20% indicating opposition. Individuals in the thirty to forty-nine age group are the least in favor of such programs regardless of education or gender, perhaps because they and their children are the most threatened by the possibility of "reverse discrimination." Nonetheless, there is widespread Jewish support for helping disadvantaged groups as long as the programs do not employ quotas (Cohen, 1982).

Among the important measures of "liberalism" is the willingness to live next door to or personally interact with individuals from other racial, ethnic, and religious groups. The great majority of Los Angeles Jews say it makes no difference who their neighbors are, yet an analysis of attitudes and behavior toward various cultural groups points to very substantial differences. The data indicate that 83.6% have visited a white Gentile home in the past three months, but there is a sharp decline to 28.2% for visiting blacks, 28.3 percent for Mexican-Americans/Chicanos, and 29.5% for Asians. Younger, less-educated Jewish men and women are much more likely to have visited a black home; with Mexican-Americans, it is younger, less-educated Jewish men who are more interactive; and for Asians, both educated and less-educated Jews under fifty are the most likely to mingle. In spite of these variations, it is well to remember that much more personal contact takes place between Jews and various minorities than occurs with minorities and other white groups.

With respect to attitudes toward living next door to members of particular groups, most Jews say they don't care. Yet a closer assessment shows there are some preferences with respect to certain cultures, especially a very strong desire to live next door to other Jews. Italians and Asians are a distant second choice, and there is less interest shown toward living next to Catholics, blacks, Mexican-Americans, white Southerners, or Arabs. This suggests that whatever biases exist pertain as much to cultural and geographical differences as they do to race and ethnicity (see Table 55). On balance, while Jews do express preferences for certain groups, they tend to be more open, involved, and supportive of minorities than are other whites.

Survivalism has been defined in the context of the recent turning inward of Los Angeles Jews to a primary, if not exclusive, concern with issues affecting the Jewish interest. Certainly this is true of a substantial segment of the Jewish community and many of its leaders, but it does not describe the multifaceted interests of most Jews who are indeed committed to Jewish survival, but who continue to be concerned with the health and vigor of this pluralistic democratic society. The Los Angeles Jewish experience is a case in point with a very high proportion still believing and behaving as if social idealism is a crucial aspect of being Jewish.

In recent years, Jews have been described somewhat simplistically as moving to the right because of their revulsion against the New Left, racial tensions, and the fear of crime. Although the anxiety of Jews and others about civic instability has produced a new mood of social realism, Jews continue to vote against candidates of the right and in support of those who seek to advance the interests of Jews and the well-being of all. This is perceived as being in harmony with the ethical content of Judaism and is often translated into social activism and liberalism in politics. But Los

TABLE 55

PREFERENCES REGARDING LIVING NEXT DOOR TO PEOPLE OF VARIOUS BACKGROUNDS

Preference	Asian	Black	Catholic	Arabic	Jewish	Mexican American/ Chicano	Italian	White Southerner
Like	12.4	6.5	6.1	4.8	44.7	6.5	12.5	6.8
Not like	6.1	24.5	5.6	41.2	0.9	28.6	4.2	22.9
Doesn't matter	79.8	66.5	87.1	52.0	53.4	63.3	82.1	67.9
No opinion	1.7	2.5	1.2	2.0	1.0	1.6	1.2	2.4
	100.0%	100.0%	100.0%	100.0%	100.0%	100.0%	100.0%	100.0%

Angeles Jews who become involved in the struggles of others are displaying a new sense of pride in their Jewishness and are identifying themselves as members of a group that has also suffered oppression.

Jewish identification has moved to a focus on the social, economic, and ethnic interests of the group that is reflected in the shift from a religious to an ethnic-cultural self-description. Most Los Angeles Jews have experienced some anti-Semitism and discrimination, and they are responding with renewed political awareness and activism. There is a profound concern with extremism of the left and the right and very little interest in supporting radicalism or Socialism.

The expanding and successful involvement of Los Angeles Jews in American politics is reflected in a sense of political cohesiveness and assertiveness that has carried them into the City Council and Board of Supervisors in Los Angeles, the California Legislature and the U.S. Congress. This suggests that it is not powerlessness that is the major threat to Jewish survival. While responses to attacks against Jews are a necessary aspect of the quest for Jewish continuity, there is a need to move beyond survivalism to a new understanding and consciousness of the meaning of Jewish life. Social liberalism will also not be enough to assure a Jewish future, especially as Jews enter the comforts of the middle class and become more troubled and uncertain than in the past. These complex and shifting patterns underscore the importance of redefining the purposes and conditions of Jewish life on a continuum from ethical excellence to Judaic commitment, so that an all-embracing Jewish community will reflect the varied and changing aspirations of Jews today.

VIII

Conclusions and Policy Implications

Teachings in Torah and Halacha have given meaning and direction to Jewish life over many centuries, providing a framework for the spiritual needs of Jews as well as their daily activities. In modern times, there have been significant challenges to Jewish traditions, as cultural changes stimulated by the Emancipation as well as by the emergence of science and rationalism have led to growing skepticism and a general decline in religious interest. This process has been reinforced by the enormous freedom enjoyed by American Jews who have experienced unprecedented opportunities for mobility and assimilation.

The changing patterns of current Jewish behavior are reflected in a decline of affiliation, observance, Jewish education, and fertility and an upturn in divorce, intermarriage, and alternate lifestyles. The Los Angeles Jewish community and others throughout the country are responding to these concerns through various processes of self-examination aimed at discovering new and improved ways of strengthening individual identity and group commitment. Religious leaders, scholars, officials of community organizations, and people of all ages and classes are seeking to understand how they can have a meaningful Jewish life in a plural society where Jews have advanced significantly but are still impacted by prejudice and discrimination.

Jews in Los Angeles and elsewhere are functioning in a post-Emancipation mode in which they are still adjusting to the modern world. American society places a premium on conformity and mobility so that the maintenance of individual and group identity is increasingly difficult. A sense of anxiety and uncertainty pervades the conscious and unconscious thoughts of Jews as they react to anti-Israel hostility, threats to world Jewry, and their perceived lack of full acceptance in American culture. But the greatest danger to Jewish continuity may well be the disintegration from within that is underscored by apathy, alienation, and indifference, as well as by a significant degree of acculturation that tends to dissolve Jewish ties and loyalties.

At the same time, there are many signs of Jewish vitality and commitment marked by various forms of religious expression as well as by a new and powerful assertiveness on behalf of Jewish needs and interests. Jewish "survivalists" are taking the lead in manifesting concern with assimilation and the importance of a Jewish future through a philosophical and programmatic outlook focused on Jewish pride and participation, along with an emphasis on the mutual responsibility of Jews, tzedakah, and Jewish empowerment. This is underscored by a sense of activism as well as a determination to use politics and protest in the quest for Jewish security. The "never again" point of view of the Jewish Defense League has been accepted by many Jews, even while they deplore the methods it uses.

The core element of Jewish survivalism is a commitment to the security and future of Israel. But the Jews of Los Angeles, indeed Jews throughout this country, have no intention of moving to Israel even as they view it as central to their Jewishness. There is little acceptance of the Zionist view that life in the American diaspora is Jewishly unfulfilling, unauthentic, and temporary. Indeed, Los Angeles Jewry tend to believe that a healthy and creative Jewish life is possible here, and they view their support for Israel in terms of their shared values as Jews and as Americans. While there has been some disillusionment and emotional slippage resulting from certain unpopular actions of the government of Israel, the ongoing view of American Jews is that ties to Israel not only strengthen Jewish life but are largely consistent with the national interest of the United States.

A substantial majority of Los Angeles Jews have experienced some prejudice and discrimination, and perceive a danger to Jews from extremist groups of the right and the left. This view is grounded in the political attacks against Israel and American Jews who come to its defense, as well as the continuation of anti-Jewish vandalism and terrorism around the world. At the same time, there are the objective realities of greater acceptance of Jews in all walks of life and the fact that there is no government sanction or political base for anti-Semitism in America. In many respects, Jews in this country have never had it so good, yet they are more anxious and worried today than they have been for some time. One of the reasons that Holocaust education has gained such acceptance among Jews is the underlying fear that it could happen again.

Although Jews are maintaining their support for social justice, human rights, and efforts to aid the disadvantaged, there has been a shift from the liberal-left orientation of the past to one that emphasizes social change in the context of moderation and civic stability. But there is also endorsement of the fight against crime, drug abuse, and those social pathologies that often disrupt family life. In a sense, Jews are moving toward a new and less ideological perception of their place in American culture that stresses respect for diversity and personal freedom while challenging the threats of social disruption. They are seeking to preserve the moral order and to protect democratic values through their participation in the social, cultural, and political structures of our pluralistic society.

The perceived "melting pot" of Los Angeles has not destroyed Jewish identification, and new forms of collective participation and involvement have been created. Jews have worked out a system of cultural pluralism that facilitates the assocation of family and friends in the primary group while encouraging full participation in the economic, political, and civic aspects of the secondary and tertiary groups. Although many Jews have moved away from traditional involvement in the religious and cultural structures of the Jewish community, they have found new ways to deal with the need for Jewish identification in an impersonal and sometimes unfriendly environment.

Jewish identification among the Jews of Los Angeles is becoming less a form of tribalism than a search for meaning and purpose in life. In our highly mobile and diverse community, Jewish identity is shifting away from religion, language, and organizations to the social, economic, and ethnic interests of the group. There are varied expressions of religious, communal, and private Jewish behavior, but self-definition of what it means to be a Jew has become an overriding characteristic of Los Angeles Jewry. Whether affiliated or not, most Jews are affected in varying degrees by the processes of acculturation as they find their own unique ways of expressing themselves Jewishly.

Young people searching for a meaningful Jewish life and Jewish values represent a generally untapped reservoir of Jewish communal strength. Among fourth generation Jews in Los Angeles, the great-grandchildren of the immigrants, there is a growing Jewish awareness and activism, more religious and communal participation and a concern for a Jewish future that has taken on the qualities of a Jewish revival. The prospects for Jewish survival are reinforced by the gravitational pull of Israel which is seen by some as a source of spiritual enrichment and pride and by others as the center of a Copernican Jewish world.

Many Jews of all ages are out of touch with Jewish organizations and practice, and have moved from religious identification to an ethnic-cultural self-perception. Jewish identity has declined over time, but it continues to be strong as Jews seek a balance between being Jewish and being like others. For most Jews in Los Angeles and elsewhere, Jewish identity is defined by their ethnicity and life-style as well as by the quest for rootedness, unique values, and traditions. Their American and Jewish identities differ yet overlap, as they develop ethnic, national, and cultural forms that tend to supplant religion. This is the special challenge of living in a predominantly Christian and increasingly secular environment, neither of which is conducive to the formation and maintenance of Jewish identity.

A number of Jews have come to the Los Angeles area from other parts of the country and from Europe because of political oppression and economic opportunities as well as the pleasant climate. The move has been accompanied by some loss of ethnic contact and involvement, especially in this large geographical setting where people often live near their work rather than near their kin. The abandonment of Jewish neighborhoods and the separation of individuals from family and friends has adversely affected the maintenance of Jewish identity that, in the past, was facilitated by geographic concentration. While there were and are some Jewish enclaves in different parts of the metropolitan area, the tendency is for individuals and families to disperse. Among these are some persons for whom the migration to California represents an opportunity to assimilate into the larger culture in order to lose an identity that no longer meets their needs. For most Jews, however, there is a desire to reestablish some Jewish connections as an underpinning of their individual and communal identity.

In this process, Jews have moved from the central and eastern areas of Los Angeles to the San Fernando Valley and the west side. A new migration is taking Jews to outlying places so that only one-third now live in areas of heavy Jewish concentration, but some are returning to the heavily Jewish urban core. The migration to Los Angeles of people from other parts of the country as well as from Israel, Iran, and the Soviet Union has added to the burgeoning population and to the complexity of an already differentiated community.

The free-wheeling, diverse, sprawling environment of Los Angeles preceded the suburban milieu that developed elsewhere a generation or more later. What has emerged is the "psychological" enclave that is no longer based on neighboring, and calls for new ways to maintain group cohesiveness and commitment. To facilitate ethnic communication, new modes of ingroup association are now required in order to preserve friendships and extended family ties over a wide area. Friends and families are connected by the automobile, the telephone, and the media, as well as by the religious, cultural, charitable, and social institutions of the Jewish community.

In spite of the continued movement of Jews to Los Angeles, the total population is no longer growing. This is a consequence of the postponement of marriage, the growing incidence of divorce, separation, widowhood, higher levels of intermarriage, and lower rates of fertility. The trend is reinforced by the increasing participation of women in higher education and in the work force, factors that contribute to an upturn in the number of single adults. Although Jews still place a high value on marriage and the family, the direction is toward new living arrangements, fewer children, and an aging population.

The changing values and lifestyles of Jews are manifested in the growth of teenage and adult interdating that is contributing to a sharp increase in intermarriage. Parents teach their children to believe in egalitarianism and democratic ideals, and there is a consequent lack of resistance to and approval of intermarriage. Women, older Jews, and the affiliated are the most opposed to intermarriage, but a majority of all Jews are accepting and even positive in their responses.

In marriages where no conversion takes place, it is much more difficult to transmit Jewish norms and values. Intermarried couples tend to have fewer children, are less likely to raise them as Jews, and these children themselves are more likely to intermarry. When there is a conversion to Judaism, however, participation in Jewish communal and religious life is comparable to that of endogamous marriages; there is a similarity in birth rates and such marriages tend to be happy. The reality is that Jews are more and more emphasizing love and self-fulfillment and there is less stigma attached to intermarriage.

There are many Jewish subcommunities and trends in Jewish life, as Jews react to the increasing rates of social, psychological, and cultural change in a technological society. Individualism and privatism are prevalent along with an emphasis on the self and personal needs and a corresponding reduction of reponsibility to the group and society. But many people of all ages, especially the young, recognize the emptiness of private pursuits and self-gratification, and search for their identity and roots in the Jewish religio-cultural-ethnic environment.

Jewish identity is very difficult to define because of the great diversity that has characterized Jewish life throughout history. The Jewish religious civilization of the past did not distinguish between nationality, culture, and religion, and there were always aspects of acculturation and accomodation in the various societies in which Jews resided. Today, there are religious, cultural, and secular Jews whose attitudes and behavior toward being Jewish range from commitment to assimilation. Yet there are commonalities for most Jews whose Jewish identity is kept alive by ethnic values and experiences including the powerful impact of Israel, the memory of the Holocaust, ongoing anti-Semitism, and a sense of peoplehood.

Major changes are taking place in Jewish identification in the context of American pluralism. In Los Angeles as elsewhere, Judaism is grounded more in a communal than in a religious orientation, with many attaching themselves to Jewish symbols, social networks, and the struggle to protect Jewish interests. They tend to acculturate rather than assimilate while retaining their identity, communal structures, and a sense of group solidarity. Jewish identity is now defined through giving, belonging, and life experiences with other Jews, rather than solely in terms of religious identification.

The Jewish family is the basic unit of Jewish socialization and identity formation, as children incorporate the values, attitudes, and beliefs of parents. Ethnic practices, rituals, and ceremonies contribute to a clear and positive feeling of belonging especially in homes that are emotionally stable and supportive. Identity is formed in both conscious and unconscious ways and represents the internalization of various identifications that combine inherited qualities with the series of environments encountered in life.

Jewish identity is reflected in the unique ways in which Jews see themselves, relate to others, and interact with society. Those who identify positively tend to have a high self-esteem, but others have been adversely affected by the perception that some groups are valued more than Jews. This has contributed to feelings of inferiority and anxiety, as Jews are more and more isolated from the protection of extended families and communal institutions. The kinship systems that were developed when Jews lived in ghettos and in isolation are less available to provide the support that used to come from the community and its formal and informal structures.

Still, Jews of all ages and backgrounds have moved away from many of the negative experiences and conflicts of the past into a more hospitable and accepting modern world. In Los Angeles and elsewhere, Jews find an open, diverse environment that permits freedom of expression and religion while assuring the rights of full citizenship. Despite ongoing manifestations of prejudice, they are able to participate more or less fully in the life of the community through their individual initiative, creative ability, and communal generosity.

As the second largest Jewish community in the United States, Los Angeles is now a major center of Jewish cultural, religious, and educational forms so that it is extraordinarily representative of Jewish life everywhere. In the past, Los Angeles tended to have a communal inferiority complex because it was perceived as suffering from cultural lag and nonconformist behavior. Today the Jewish community of Los Angeles is a pioneering force and a leader in Jewish affairs here and abroad. Its institutional systems provide a strong underpinning for an exciting, dynamic, and changing Jewish community.

The Jews of Los Angeles are also deeply involved in serving the total community through their active participation in its social, economic, political, and civic life. Increasing numbers of Jews are elected to public office, serve on governmental commissions, and provide leadership in cultural and intellectual affairs. The bastions of privilege and power from which Jews have been barred are slowly changing, and there are now few places from which they are excluded. Jews are found increasingly in the executive suites and on the boards of major corporations and banks, and they are now being admitted to clubs that used to discriminate against them.

Still, there is a high level of uncertainty and anxiety among all generations of Los Angeles Jewry regarding the meaning of being a Jew in a plural society. The various generations share the commonality of Jewish history, religion, and culture, but there are experiential and attitudinal differences among them. None of the generations is homogeneous, with some acculturating more rapidly than others. At the same time, a number of people have turned inward and reinforced their Jewishness by withdrawing from public life into the psychological realm where they search for personal meaning. This has led to an emphasis on human relationships and feelings, sometimes in the context of observance and tradition.

While the first generation sought to adjust to a new culture with its different language, behavior, and expectations, the second generation struggled with two cultures, the world of their parents and that of the land in which they were born. Because of the ambivalence of the second generation, their children were not adequately equipped to deal with Jewishness and tried to find a personal identity by developing new careers, moving to different places, and creating alternate lifestyles. The material success of the third generation has made it possible for the fourth to have the time and leisure for self-examination and self-renewal. Thus, a fourth generation Jewish renewal is occurring as many young Jews seek to overcome the normlessness and alienation of society in the context of their need for Jewish roots and communal ties.

The renaissance of Jewish interest among fourth generation Jews is a selective one in which ethnic-cultural Jewishness has tended to supplant religion as a self-defining charcteristic of Jewish identity. A sense of peoplehood is stronger in this generation and is carried on through kinship, friends, organizational ties, and concern for Jews everywhere. Their cultural identity is expressed in Jewish art, literature, music, language, and theater. Strong Jewish beliefs and practices are especially prevalent among those who came from families involved in Jewish life and whose parental homes were characterized by a warm and supportive emotional climate. These are the individuals who are most likely to join Jewish organizations and raise their children Jewishly, and they give support to the view that a meaningful Jewish experience can be anticipated in later generations.

But aggregate statistics sometimes hide the trends within groups, and there is another fourth generation consisting of young Jews who are rapidly assimilating into the larger culture. Most of these individuals are unaffiliated with any Jewish institution, are far less interested in Jewish affairs, and reflect high levels of Jewish illiteracy. Even within this subgroup, however, there are those who have a strong residue of Jewish identity and are looking for something human and Jewish to which they can attach themselves in an impersonal, fragmented, and uncaring society. These persons represent a significant resource for a Jewish future, and it is essential to overcome the communal tendency to dismiss them from corporate Jewish life.

Voluntary organizations were created in the religious and communal spheres to help meet certain personal needs and to assure the survival of the group. Los Angeles Jews have developed a complex, differentiated system of institutions for the spiritual, cultural, educational, and social welfare requirements of their community. The philanthropic world of Jews in Los Angeles is a central focus of Jewish life through which religious beliefs, organizational objectives, and social needs are met. Pressures exist to encourage Jewish communal involvement in fund raising and synagogue membership, and Jewish country clubs require their prospective members to support Jewish activities. Parents join temples and synagogues to provide their children with a Jewish education, and Jewish centers, youth groups, and other organizations offer social and cultural activities as well as mutual aid for those in need. Jewish Los Angeles is an organization-centered community whose culture is practiced through various organizations and away from the home.

However, fewer than half of the Jews in Los Angeles belong to either a congregation or a Jewish communal organization, a sharp decline both from their own previous behavior as well as from the experience of their parents. Some of the unaffiliated act out their Jewishness through social and family networks, supporting Israel and Jewish interests in the political arena, and even expressing various forms of religiosity. A substantial proportion are people who find memberships too expensive because they are at the lower margins of the economy including older Jews, the young, divorced, single-parent families, and others who are not part of the culture of affluence. Some do not join for other reasons including apathy, indifference, the feeling of being unwelcome in families where there has been an intermarriage, and the belief that institutional Judaism does not offer meaningful programs relevant to their lives.

There is more emphasis on organizational and philanthopic obligations than on religious devotion and traditional religious discipline among the Jews of Los Angeles. A decline is evident in ritual and attendance, as Jews selectively observe seders, Sabbath candle lighting, fasting on Yom Kippur, and attendance at high holiday services. Relgious obligations that take the least time and effort are the most likely to be observed, and there is much support for passive and symbolic practices such as owning a menorah or Bible, or placing a mezuzah on a door frame.

Still, there are hopeful signs of a renewed interest in various forms of Judaism many of which are steeped in Halacha. For a considerable number of Jews, including some young persons of the fourth generation, the synagogue is once again becoming an all-encompassing institution for observance, prayer, and political and social activities. The general move away from Jewish structures is challenged by the reemergence of congregations as subcommunities as well as religious associations in which Jews join together to meet their spiritual and communal needs in a religious setting. Today, Los Angeles has a large number of synagogues and temples in which many thousands of Jews carry on the customs and beliefs of the Jewish faith.

While participation tends to define the limits of the Jewish community, the non-affiliation of a majority of the Jews in Los Angeles does not mean they are bad Jews. Many of the unaffiliated are very Jewishly oriented and religious, with a considerable proportion even more so than some of the affiliated. But others are indifferent to traditional modes of religious and communal expression and seek differing ways of identifying themselves as Jews. Although these individuals are outside of Jewish institutional life, they should not be rejected because they represent a possible reservoir of new ideas and creative forms in their havurot, communes, and even humanist activities. Young Jews particularly are confronting the relevance of

Jewish structures and their inability to answer questions about the fundamental needs of contemporary life. Their input is urgently needed in developing a balance between tradition and innovation as Jews continue to adjust to the processes of modernization.

Jewish groups must develop programs that will help large numbers of unaffiliated Jews feel a part of a Jewish communal organism without immediately having to join its institutions. This presents a serious challenge to synagogues, Jewish centers, Jewish schools, and other communal organizations that ask for financial support from the unaffiliated in order to pay for services rendered. Some institutions offer free or reduced fee memberships for those in need who seek greater involvement in religious, communal, and educational programs, but many people feel uncomfortable about taking what is perceived as charity. A number of congregations make their supplementary programming available to non-members, including activities for youth, senior citizens, and single parents. Weddings and Passover seders are also provided for those who can demonstrate their need, but tickets for the high holidays are generally sold in order to generate useful revenue. Synagogues that have nursery schools tend to permit children of non-members to attend, but a higher fee is generally charged. The one area that is usually closed to the unaffiliated is the religious school, so that Jewish education tends to be accessible only for those who belong.

Most Jews would agree with the concept that no one should be denied participation in religious services or refused social assistance from a Jewish agency because of an inability to pay. Despite numerous efforts to deal with these matters, however, the problem remains largely unresolved. What should be given more serious consideration is the premise that membership in religious and communal institutions is the birthright of every Jew. This would still allow for freedom of choice because an individual could "opt out" of the community rather than "opt in" as is the case now. It would tend to encourage greater participation in Jewish life and help to create a new mindset about Jewish participation in a plural society. The necessary financial support could be forthcoming from the "pyramid-type" fund raising employed by the United Jewish Welfare Fund, with those most able to contribute asked to be even more generous and others unable to give permitted to do so when and if their financial situations allow.

Such a policy would recognize the religious, cultural, recreational, and social welfare needs of the entire Jewish population regardless of affiliation. It would also be an expression of interest in those least able to pay dues and provide a potential source of strength for a more inclusive and responsive organized Jewish community. A question might be raised about families taking advantage of this new spirit of communal generosity, but the reality is that a considerable portion of the unaffiliated are individuals and families with financial problems who are now effectively priced out of Jewish life. Given the opportunity, most Jews will ultimately give some funds to the institutions in which they participate, as is the case in other religious communities where people at all income levels tend to be voluntarily supportive of their churches and charities.

There are various underrepresented constituencies in organized Jewish life including women, singles, young people, divorced, poor, and elderly Jews. These are the groups that lack power and access in Jewish communal structures, so that those who are the most alone are the least connected. Despite the rhetoric of inclusion, the trend in Jewish institutions is toward centralism and elitism, and community planning has become a euphemism for the control of Jewish systems by limited numbers of people. The unaffiliated are asked to join Jewish organizations and take advantage of opportunities for developing policies and programs. Few of those who seek to do so are meaningfully involved in decision making, and others make little or no effort to gain influence because they do not believe it is readily available to them.

There is long-standing hostility and opposition to the acceptance in Jewish life of the intermarried, converts to Judaism, and even their children. The danger today is that the Jewish community is being split into theologically separate groups according to the different Halachic interpretations of who is a Jew. The Jewishness of thousands is being contested and, with the rise of intermarriage, these numbers are growing dramatically. A demographic disaster for Jewish survival may be in the offing unless new forms of dialogue can be created within the Jewish community to address the issue. For this purpose, the approach of the National Jewish Resource Center to intra-Jewish ecumenism (Greenberg, 1985) must be applied in Los Angeles and elsewhere.

The intermarried and their children along with young, educated Jews and women represent primary targets of opportunity for involvement in Jewish life. There are large numbers of young, committed, socially motivated Jews who need to be offered more roles and a freer hand in leading Jewish organizations. Women tend to have a stronger sense of Jewish identity than men and should be more fully utilized in positions of communal responsibility. Los Angeles Jews are generally accepting of women in a minyan or as rabbis, but few women have moved into authoritative communal situations. Expanded programs are needed for all of these groups such as a "buddy" system to make newcomers welcome, low-cost day care with Jewish content for the children of working women, and activities that reflect the social concerns of the young. Above all, there should be a recognition that many of the unaffiliated are shy, lonely people who are frightened by communal structures and for whom a personal and human outreach is essential.

Strengthening Jewish commitment and the transmission of a positive Jewish identity are primary issues for Jewish groups today. Their concern is motivated by the dramatic changes taking place in the Jewish family that has long been the critical vehicle for Jewish survival. Problems in the Jewish family are growing with fewer viable or intact, and more services are needed for singles, the elderly, divorcees, single-parent families, and those with alternate lifestyles. New policies and programs can help to reemphasize the importance of the stable family now being stressed by societal and cultural influences that tend to change traditional patterns.

While maintaining contact with Jewish singles, it is important to encourage their interest in the long-standing Jewish values of marriage and raising a family. They will need assistance in quality day care, Jewish education for their children, and programs that help them to experience Jewishness as a unit. There is a need for coordination of counseling and referral services for individuals and families, family life education courses, better utilization of seniors as surrogate grandparents, and improved outreach through paraprofessionals and agency volunteers. It is also necessary to develop programs that help to maintain multi-generational families in stable neighborhoods through shifts in the multiplicity of government policies that adversely affect the ability of families to function in the present economy.

Those who do not make use of Jewish services require assistance in making a connection with the organized Jewish community as a means of dealing with personal identity crises in the private sphere. The Jewish agency can serve as a buffer between the individual and the family on the one hand and the larger society on the other. It is a vital institutional link that can help to develop a sense of community for individual Jews by combatting alienation and anomie. Since large numbers of Jews are out of touch with Jewish organizations, radio and television programs and Jewish cable TV can be extremely important in the processes of communicating to the uninvolved and needy the interest of a caring and open Jewish community. A 24-hour Jewish communal "hotline" is crucial, so that persons who need help or wish to make Jewish contacts have a central source of advice and information.

At a time when geographical mobility and economic dislocation undermine family cohesion and Jewish communal life, new ways must be found to assist those who have moved and lost the supporting structures of family, friends, and neighborhoods. Referral services are needed for Jews who move from one community to another with data about housing and Jewish communal services, and newcomers to communities should receive credit for membership fees and building assessments paid to former congregations. Perhaps, most important, are the havurot and fellowship groupings that can offer shared Jewish experiences and mutual social support. Along with satellite services brought to places with new populations, the warmth and interest of other Jews extended on a personal basis is a primary factor in creating ties to those who wish to have a sense of Jewish belonging.

There has been much concern about the perceived failure of Jewish education to hold back the tide of assimilation or to reverse the erosion of Jewish identity among young people. But it is likely that social and demographic trends including changes in the character of the family have had a more powerful impact in the formation of Jewish identity. Nonetheless, Jewish education does have a responsibility for developing among young people a healthy sense of their Jewish identity and positive attitudes toward the continuity of the Jewish people. This goes beyond gaining knowledge in specific content areas and pertains to the attitudes of students toward Judaism and the Jewish community.

It is unfortunate that the experiences of many young people in Jewish schools and educational programs tend to reduce and weaken their Jewish commitment. Jewish education can alienate and repel children because it is often joyless, authoritarian, and irrelevant to their real-life experiences. Much of the responsibility rests with the parents who do not instill in their children any appreciation of Jewish values or culture. They turn to the schools to create a sense of Jewish identity in their children, but the process fails because even the best schools are unable to do the job in a family and communal vacuum.

Most of the schools are part-time and supplementary so that children receive very limited exposure to Jewish history, culture, and religious values. Another problem is that some teachers and administrators are themselves inadequately educated and prepared, but this is changing because the Los Angeles Bureau of Jewish Education, Jewish institutions of higher learning, and various national bodies are developing improved standards, curricula, and training programs. Since the influences of the family and community are also important in shaping a positive Jewish identity, the organized Jewish community is placing a high value on the re-Judaization of the home through family-oriented education and various youth-related experiences such as Jewish camping and programs in Israel.

There is a significant increase in the number of day schools and the students who attend them, but more time has to be made available for improved supplementary education to help prepare young Jews to function Jewishly in a pluralistic society. A balance is needed between the cognitive and affective goals of Jewish education, with an emphasis on providing experiences and an environment conducive to Jewish learning and identity formation. The promotion of adult education programs, syllabi for home study, and scholarship aid are crucial aspects of efforts to reach that part of the population not touched by existing programs.

There is also a need to aggressively promote Jewish study and reading among the large reservoir of potentially interested Jews through Jewish book clubs, groups that discuss issues presented in Jewish journals, the use of the media for Jewish learning and outreach, and even the popularization of Jewish holidays in a "Golden Books" type of literature that can be sold in supermarkets. Supplementary education has to be made more relevant and appealing to young people, and programs must tap into the rich resources of Israel. Jewish singles and young married retreats should be subsidized at places such as the Brandeis-Bardin Institute to encourage the young to a new sense of Jewish pride and interaction.

Throughout history, Jews have reinterpreted their identity in terms of various ideological and cultural challenges. Profound adjustments in Jewish life were already taking place before the fall of the Jewish commonwealth in the diaspora centers of Babylon, Alexandria, and Rome. These Jewish communities and others helped to save and perpetuate Judaism by learning from the majority societies in which they lived. The ability of Jews to absorb and transmit the best ideas and experiences of other cultures helped them to grow as a people while continuing the core values of the Jewish tradition. At the same time, Jews helped to shape the various physical, social, and political environments in which they lived.

Whether consciously or not, American Jews are now involved in a process of creating a new Jewish civilization in which secularism is confronting religious tradition. Freedom and the lack of restrictions have facilitated the diversification of Jewish life as American Judaism interacts significantly with other strains of modern culture. One of the important consequences has been the emergence of secular approaches that challenge traditional views. In the move away from religious authority, a new synthesis is emerging that is defined by the cross-fertilization of the sacred and the secular (Potok, 1978).

Today, the Jewish community is developing in a multiplicity of ways that have varying degrees of validity and meaning for a Jewish future. There is an elite religious group maintaining very high standards of religious and cultural expression and there are others who are largely uninvolved and disinterested. A folk religious group is engaged in practices on an acculturated basis, and a secular group is committed to the ethnic and cultural survival of the Jewish people. Both the religious and the non-religious aspects of Jewish expression are needed and serve as terminals on a continuum that helps to orient and maintain Jewish life.

There is a tendency to label as assimilationists all Jews who do not measure up to a standard of Jewish identification that includes both Judaism as a faith and Jewishness as an ethnic identity. The limitation of this perspective is that it excludes from Jewish life those who are not attracted to religious institutions or whose Jewish emotional ties are not yet clearly defined. Little help is available to many young people who are seeking self-fulfillment in new and non-traditional ways or to those who choose secular humanism as the moral and intellectual embodiment of their Jewishness. This is not to suggest that the Jewish tradition should be abandoned but, rather, that there needs to be a search for constructive alternatives that will be more Jewishly inclusive.

There are a dozen different Judaisms with various visions, adherents, and promises of fulfillment. Who is to decide which is better? What we share is a sense of community that involves memories, myths, traditions, and commitments. What we need is a balance between our ethical and ethnic commitments as Jews, a dialectic between Jewish universalism and particularism. An increased intellectual understanding of those perspectives on life that are uniquely Jewish can facilitate a commitment to the Jewish community even from those who are theological agnostics but who can accept a Jewish moral or ethical perspective.

Jews are seeking to determine whether being Jewish means having Jewish friends or whether it also means having a set of values and a special outlook on God, man, and the world. They are deciding whether they want to be merely a social group in the guise of a religious group or a people moved by a particular religious and cultural heritage. If it is the latter, it requires a great deal of knowledge and understanding of Jewish law and lore. It is also necessary to make Jewish survival a worthwhile goal by substituting Jewish affirmations and satisfactions for the negative feelings and frustrations that Jews have faced over the years. Of particular importance are the great ideas and ideals uniquely created by Jews as their contribution to civilization, including the notions of human equality and a belief in a monotheistic God.

A number of Jewish religious leaders, educators, sociologists, and others feel that Jews in America cannot maintain themselves without distinctiveness—both public and private. Today, Jews express themselves publicly by supporting Israel politically, contributing to the United Jewish Appeal, to their congregations, and communal groups. But this public identification does not affect their personal lifestyle, commitment, and the ways in which they express themselves every day. Many feel that Jews will not remain Jewish unless their Jewishness affects them in a very personal and meaningful manner. It is out of the creative spirit of individual Jews rather than Jewish institutions alone that the processes of Jewish renewal and self-definition will emerge.

While the potential for renewal resides in the Jewish people, Jewish institutions are essential to structure and carry forward the values and traditions of the Jewish experience. Jewish culture is parceled out to a number of organizations with religion under the auspices of the synagogue, fighting anti-Semitism done by community relations groups, and recreation under the auspices of community centers or a country club. Jews have created networks of religious and communal institutions that help to resist massive assimilation, while extensive acculturation continues to take place. But while Jewish organizations and their activities are the collective embodiment of Jewish culture, Jewishness itself continues in private conduct, manner, and style, as well as through ideas and morals. It is personal honesty, compassion, advocacy of justice, and mercy that help individual Jews move toward Jewish meaning.

There is a need for a new ideology of American Jewish life that looks more to the future. It must go beyond the approaches of despair and lamentation so common among Jewish leaders today and recognize that Jews have friends, influence, and a certain amount of power. A remarkable resurgence of Jewish interest has taken place in recent years that portends well for the rest of the century. This involves a sense of historical perspective that points to the maintenance of a high level of Jewish identity and creativity.

In order to sustain and enrich Jewish civilization, the Jewish community must go beyond the doctrine of "survivalism" and give meaning and support to various modes of Jewish experience. While Jews can be perfectionists in setting standards for themselves, it is important to recognize the Jewish vitality in this country that touches every aspect of Jewish life. There is a renaissance in Jewish theology, philosophy, the social sciences, and Jewish humanities, and Jewish religious and communal institutions have been recreated and improved upon. Jewish writers are among the best in American literature and are writing about Jewish themes that teach the Gentile world a great deal about Jewish culture. And significant numbers of young Jews accept and are comfortable with their own Jewishness and are participating in Jewish studies programs. The recurring question of why they should remain Jewish is being answered through identification with the past of the Jewish people, a belief in a shared destiny, and a messianic ingredient in which Jews seek a more perfect world and a place in achieving it.

The Holocaust and the creation of Israel underscore the importance of an ideology of defense that has become for many a metaphysical and historical perception of their Jewish consciousness. Israel reinforces American Jewish ethnicity as well as an appreciation of Jewish culture, and it is important to stress areas of collaborative activity that require mutual respect and an acknowledgement of the legitimacy of both communities. But an Israeli-based American Jewishness does not provide an adequate answer for life in the diaspora. Israel offers a meaningful focus for Jewish unity and emotion, but Jews in this country live in a pluralistic world in which the challenges of particularism and universalism must be faced continually. American Jews do not live in nor are they likely to live in a totally Jewish environment, so that exclusive reliance on the ideology of survivalism defined in Jewish nationalistic terms is unrealistic.

The liberty Jews enjoy in the United States means having the right to a religious, cultural, and corporate freedom that enhances the Jewish heritage. It also involves a sense of responsibility for the welfare of democratic society as a whole, including the strengthening of its institutions and a commitment to social justice and human rights. Jews have an important role to play through their uniquely cosmopolitan understanding of blended cultures that has been an important characteristic of the Jewish leavening of the western intellectual tradition.

The ultimate need is not only Jewish group survival, but meaningful survival that comes from identification with others with whom there is a sharing of mutual interests and values. This process of renewal will help Jews to strengthen the links of Jewish peoplehood everywhere, while they deepen their attachments to America. They have a major stake in the future of this country and feel a profound obligation to contribute to its well-being. It is here that Jews have found political equality, religious liberty, and the opportunity to perpetuate their culture. For these reasons and others, they see a bright future in America for themselves as well as for their children and future generations.

Appendix: Methods and Procedures

A number of studies have been done on Jewish identity, but there is little consensus on what it is, how it is formed, or its future potential. The precise definition of Jewish identity has not emerged even though rabbis and Jewish social scientists indicate that such factors as birth, religion, and nationality need to be taken into account. Some researchers focus on behavioral characteristics such as affiliation, observance, Jewish education, charitable giving, and friendship patterns. Others emphasize attitudinal responses toward Israel, traditional beliefs, intermarriage, self-identification, and moral excellence. Studies of Jewish acculturation often rely on reference group theory which is based on the premise that a person's identity is most influenced by "significant others" or "reference groups." Generation, life cycle, and socioeconomic status are also examined as indicators of Jewishness and group commitment. Most researchers accept the premise that Jewish identity is a multifaceted phenomenon that goes beyond religious identification to encompass varying degrees of social and psychological attachment to the Jewish people.

The Jewish identity scale used in the interviews was developed over many months and was validated by the ratings of a nationwide panel of sixty judges on an extended battery of Jewish identity items. Jews of great prominence were included on the panel from religion, sociology, psychology, political science, Jewish education, and community organizations, representing a veritable "Who's Who" of academic and Jewish affairs. Once the replies were in, computer analysis revealed which items produced consensus and which dissensus. This led to the inclusion of thirty items in the interview schedule that was based on an ethnic identity and group cohesiveness scale and its three subconstructs of religion, culture, and peoplehood (Sandberg, 1974).

This is a summated rating scale, also known as a Likert-type scale, consisting of a number of items of approximately equal value (Murphy and Likert, 1937). A six-point scale was employed, ranging from "strongly agree" to "strongly disagree" (see Table 30). After the subject responded to the statements with varying degrees of agreement or disagreement, the scores were grouped in order to yield an individual's identity score. Categories were established to differentiate among those of high and low identity.

The measurement of the identity variables is a crucial element of the research design, and the scale seeks to measure attitudes that include a number of psychological objects. L.L. Thurstone (1928) defined an "attitude" as the degree of positive or negative effect associated with some psychological object. He described as a psychological object any symbol, phrase, idea, or institution toward which people can express positive or negative responses.

Michael Parenti (1967) observed that personality considerations are also an important factor in ethnic identification, since many individuals consciously choose to associate with others of their own background. Sigmund Freud and others, however, placed greater emphasis on the unconscious forces that exercise control over the conscious thoughts and deeds of people (Hall and Lindzey, 1970). Hence, although the ethnic scale tended to produce a series of conscious attitudinal responses, it was assumed that these replies also stemmed from the use of psychological symbols that evoked the unconscious attitudes of the respondents.

It was believed that the items selected represented the universe of interest toward which the interviewee might express varying degrees of positive or negative response. Some of the problems of other such scales were eliminated because the diverse and representative character of the panel helped to shape a broad-gauged instrument to measure Jewish identity. Particular care was taken to observe the criteria summarized by Edwards (1957) pertaining to the construction of attitude scales, including avoidance of statements that can be interpreted in more than one way, that are likely to be endorsed by everyone or no one, and that are short, direct, and clear. Some of the items were put in the negative form and later reversed in the coding process.

Questions were also written to cover the respondents' social and economic backgrounds, their personal and communal associations now and in the past, and their attitudes and behaviors on a number of variables both directly and indirectly related to Jewish life and civic concerns. These included levels of Jewish education, religious observance while growing up (with an emphasis on the teenage years), synagogue membership present and past, membership in Jewish voluntary associations, attitudes and positions regarding Israel, philanthropy, intermarriage, experience with anti-Semitism, as well as more overarching demographic characteristics such as age, sex, occupation, parental attributes and views, educational attainments, and neighborhood characteristics. Other data on integration into the larger society were also obtained including friendship patterns, residential choices, participation in non-Jewish voluntary associations, and social concerns.

With the cooperation of students from the University of California at Los Angeles (UCLA), a pretest was carried out among sixty-four respondents who live in the densely Jewish Beverly-Fairfax area. At this juncture, the interview schedule took on the average over ninety minutes to administer. This was at least one-third longer than desirable for use at the door with householders, and the schedule was reduced to approximately one hour. During the same period, the staff constructed the sampling frame, prepared the necessary record-keeping forms for the field, and wrote a field manual for interviewers that included question-by-question specifications for the use of the interview schedule. The sampling frame was composed of two elements: divisions of the Los Angeles-Long Beach Standard Metropolitan Statistical Area (i.e., "greater Los Angeles") and density of Jewish households, 1970, by Census Tract. The latter had been assessed in 1974 by researchers for the Jewish Federation Council of Greater Los Angeles.

In order to obtain a representative draw, it was determined that interviews be secured with Jewish adults in five regions (San Fernando Valley, urban core, the west side, the south, and the east) in proportion to the estimated Jewish population within each. Excluding heavily black and Spanish-surnamed Census tracts from consideration, as well as tracts in which the estimated population of Jewish households was below 5%, the remaining tracts were allocated among the five areas of the city according to Jewish density: 45% or more Jewish (dense), 15-44% Jewish (mixed), 5-14% Jewish (sparse). This resulted in a 15-cell frame, but 3 cells were empty in the south and east. The goal was to collect a representative sample of 500 Jewish adults, 18 years of age or older, out of an expected household personal canvas of more than 5,000 Jewish and non-Jewish families. After selecting tracts and blocks at random within each of the 12 cells of the frame, and apportioning interviews according to tract density, the desired number of respondents was set at 474. In a few less Jewishly dense areas, no tract sampling was required because only one tract qualified for the selection of a cell quota.

In fact, 436 interviews were conducted, but 23 householders did not sufficiently complete the interview to warrant inclusion in the analysis, leaving an N of 413. The remaining disparity results from the inability of interviewers to find any or enough Jewish adults in the areas to which they were directed. For example, the Federation Council estimates led to the expectation that Jewish households would be found in a selected Census Tract in Inglewood. Three different interviewers journeyed to the locale at three different times, but the Tract had become mostly black.

Unpaid student interviewers from UCLA received partial course credit for their participation but, subsequently, paid interviewers were recruited in order to expedite the interview process. The interviewers carried letters of introduction on both UCLA and University of Judaism letterheads which were used as needed to show the legitimacy of the project. It is impossible to determine whether or not a dwelling unit contains Jewish householders without asking for the information directly. Consequently, a series of screening questions taking a few minutes was used at each door to determine whether or not any adult Jews resided therein. The screening questionnaire begins with items that tap social and political attitudes and goes on to ask current religious affiliation as well as religion at birth. Those who were born Jews and converted to another religion were excluded from the study, while converts to Judaism were considered eligible. Once in the household, a Jewish resident was selected randomly for interviewing. Since the budget did not permit many call backs, if the randomly designated person was unavailable, the next randomly drawn person was selected.

Interviewers were called upon to canvas each and every dwelling unit in the randomly selected blocks to which they were assigned in the Census Tract under study in order to complete the desired number of interviews. Needless to state, the less densely Jewish the locale, the greater the difficulty the interviewer had in concluding the task. In each assignment within each of the selected tracts, the interviewer was bound by a sex-age quota. The interviewer was instructed to make calls evenings and weekends when it was more likely to find the more elusive respondents at home, to wit, younger, employed persons, especially men. They were successful in securing about equal proportions of men and women in the sample of 413, and good distribution by age and income. The refusal rate to the initial screening questionnaire, when to the person at the door it appeared only that a "community survey" was being done, was quite low: little more than 10%. Although it soon became apparent to potential Jewish respondents that an ample block of their time was required, refusal rates and break-offs were also quite low: little more than an additional 10%. Higher rates of refusal were encountered in some wealthier areas, especially those guarded with security gates or doormen.

The complex nature of socioeconomic conditions among Jews in Los Angeles made it important to construct a typology of socioeconomic status (SES) relevant to the current condition of ethnic groups in general and Jews in particular. This was a necessary element in the stratification and placement of individuals in the sample and facilitated the measurement of changes in Jewish cohesiveness according to socioeconomic status. Herbert Gans (1962) and August B. Hollingshead and Frederick C. Redlich (1958) agreed there are a number of different ways in which class can be defined, depending on the orientation of the researcher. Some looked at shared characteristics such as group interests and social relationships; some were concerned mainly with occupation, on the assumption that work determines access to income, power, and status, thereby influencing behavior; and others focused on an aggregate of characteristics such as education, income, occupation, and residence.

Hollingshead's Index of Social Position is premised on three assumptions that make it easier to categorize the class subcultures: (1) that social stratification exists in the community, (2) that status positions are determined mainly by a few commonly accepted cultural characteristics, and (3) that items symbolic of status may be combined to stratify the population. Consequently, a social class construct was developed which recognizes that a number of different groupings is possible according to the judgement of the researchers. The construct was based on several key variables including family income, education, and prestige of occupation.

A point system was devised to stratify the subgroups with a maximum of four points each possible for educational attainment, income and occupational prestige, or a total of 12 points. Four SES categories were created including low-low, low, high, and high-high. Consequently, the SES scores could range from a low of 3 or 4 in the low-low grouping to a high of 11 or 12 in the high-high category (see Table 56). For analytical purposes, these SES groupings were later dichotomized as high and low SES.

An index was constructed in order to differentiate among the first, second, third, and fourth generations. Those who were born outside the United States and who came to this country as immigrants were categorized as first generation. Persons who had at least one parent born abroad and who were of American nativity were grouped as second generation. The third generation consisted of individuals both of whose parents were born in the United States, but whose grandparents came from other countries. And those who had at least three of their four grandparents born in America were labeled as fourth generation.

The Jewish sensitivity index reflected the varying degrees of uneasiness expressed by the respondents when their Jewishness was exposed to public scrutiny. A six-point scale ranging from low to high sensitivity measured five items including feelings on hearing the words "Jew" or "Jewish" in mixed company, Jews being "too much" in the news, Jewish behavior in the company of Gentiles, a stranger assuming they were Jewish, and a Jew wearing a yarmulke in public. Those who were the least sensitive received 1 point for each of the five items, while the most sensitive received as many as 6 points. Out of a total possible sensitivity score of 30 points, individuals who received between 23 and 30 were considered as scoring "high" on the Jewish sensitivity scale.

A similar scoring system was used to differentiate between subgroups of Los Angeles Jews who rated high and low on five social concern items. These included attitudes toward entitlement to a minimum income, hunger and famine, full equality for all, racial discrimination, and the formation of unions. With a total possible social concern score of 30 points, those who received between 23

TABLE 56

SOCIOECONOMIC (SES) CLASSIFICATION INDEX

SES Category	Score Each Category	Education	Occupation	Annual Family Income	Total Score
Low-Low	1	Less Than High School Graduate	Any Blue Collar	Under $5,500	3-4
Low	2	High School Graduate, Some College	Sales, Clerks, Small Proprietors	$5,500 to 14,999	5-8
High	3	College Graduate	Entrepreneurs, Middle Management, Semi-Professional	$15,000 to 39,999	9-10
High-High	4	Masters Degree or Higher, Professional Degree	Professional, High Manager	$40,000 and Over	11-12

and 30 were considered as scoring "high" on the social concern index.

Both program and data-card keypunching were done without charge in the offices of Mr. William Friedland. The data were coded, checked, and cleaned during a period ending in 1979. After the materials were mounted at UCLA's Campus Computing Network, the marginals became available and multivariate analyses continued through 1985. In recognizing the possibility of a margin of error in survey research, comparisons were made with other community studies. The findings of this study are presented in the belief that they are both valid and reliable.

List of Tables

References

Ackerman, Walter I. "Jewish Education—For What?" *American Jewish Yearbook 1970*. New York and Philadelphia: American Jewish Committee and Jewish Publication Society of America, 1969.

——. "The Jewish School System in the United States." in *The Future of the Jewish Community In America*. ed. by David Sidorsky. New York: Basic Books, 1973.

Anti-Defamation League of B'nai B'rith. "1982 Audit of Anti-Semitic Incidents." New York, 1983.

Anti-Defamation League of B'nai B'rith. "1983 Audit of Anti-Semitic Incidents." New York, 1984.

American Jewish Committee. "Who is a Good Jew?" New York, 1959.

——. "Jewish Education for Modern Needs." New York, 1963.

——. "The Social Background of American Jewish Education." *The Social Context of Jewish Identity.* New York, 1972.

——. "The Jewish Poor: A Brief Bibliography." New York. July, 1973.

——. Colloquium on Jewish Education and Jewish Identity. "Summary Report and Recommendations." New York. November, 1976.

——. "Israel and American Jewish Interaction." Report of an International Task Force. New York, 1978.

——. Press Release. New York. July 17, 1980.

American Jewish Yearbook 1984. New York and Philadelphia: American Jewish Committee and the Jewish Publication Society of America, 1983.

American Jewish Yearbook 1985. New York and Philadelphia: American Jewish Committee and the Jewish Publication Society of America, 1984.

Bayer, Evan. "Jews on the Edge." New York: American Jewish Committee, 1983.

Benjamin, I. J. *Three Years in America 1859-1862*. Trans. by Charles Reznikoff. Philadelphia: Jewish Publication Society of America, 1956.

Bergman, Elihu. "The American Jewish Population Erosion." *Midstream* (October, 1977).

B'nai B'rith Messenger. (Los Angeles) December 18, 1914.

Blau, Joseph L. *Judaism in America*. Chicago: The University of Chicago Press, 1976.

Bock, Geoffrey E. "Does Jewish Schooling Matter?" *Jewish Education and Jewish Identity Colloquium Papers*. New York: American Jewish Committee, January, 1977.

Bubis, Gerald B. "The Jewish Component in Jewish Communal Service—From Theory to Practice." *Journal of Jewish Communal Service* LVI, No. 3, (Spring, 1980).

Burnham, Howard. "The Wandering Jew," *Sh'ma* 10/191, (April 4, 1980).

Clymer, Adam. "Voting Jews Remain Liberal, Poll Finds." *New York Times*. November 12, 1978.

Cohen, Steven M. *The 1984 National Survey of American Jews*. New York: American Jewish Committee, 1985.

——. "What American Jews Believe." *Moment* (July/ August, 1982).

——. "Attitudes of American Jews Toward Israel and Israelis." New York: American Jewish Committee, 1983.

——. *American Modernity and Jewish Identity*. New York and London: Tavistock Publications, 1983.

Connecticut Mutual Life Report. *American Values in the '80s: The Impact on Belief*. Hartford, Connecticut, 1981.

Dashefsky, David and Howard Shapiro. *Ethnic Identification Among American Jews*. Lexington, Massachusetts: Lexington Books, Heath, 1974.

Dawidowicz, Lucy. "A Century of Jewish History, 1881-1981: The View from America." *American Jewish Yearbook 1983*. New York and Philadelphia: American Jewish Committee and Jewish Publication Society of America, 1982.

Dorff, Elliot. "Tradition and Change in Jewish Law." *Directions* (November, 1981).

Drew, David E. et al. *A Profile of the Jewish Freshman: 1980*. Los Angeles: Higher Education Research Institute, 1981.

Dumke, Glenn S. *The Boom of the Eighties in Southern California*. San Marino: The Huntington Library, 1944.

Edwards, Allen L. *Techniques of Attitude Scale Construction*. New York: Appleton-Century-Crofts, 1957.

Elazar, Daniel J. "Decision-Making in the American Jewish Community." Philadelphia: Center for Jewish Community Studies, 1972.

Erikson, Erik H. "The Problem of Ego Identity." *Identity and Anxiety*. M. R. Stein, A. J. Vidich and D. M. White (eds.). Glencoe, Illinois: Free Press, 1960.

——. "Identity and Identity Diffusion." *The Self and Social Interaction*. C. Gordon and K. J. Gergen (eds.). New York: Wiley, 1968.

Etzioni, Amitai. "The Ghetto—A Re-evaluation." *Social Forces* 37, No. 3 (March, 1959).

Fisher, Alan, M. "Where is the New Jewish Conservatism?" *Society* 16(4)5 (May/June, 1979).

Gans, Herbert J. "American Jewry: Present and Future," *Commentary* XXI (May, 1956).

——. *The Urban Villagers*. New York: The Free Press, 1962.

——. "Symbolic Ethnicity: the Future of Ethnic Groups and Cultures in America," *On the Making of Americans: Essays in Honor of David Riesman*. Herbert J. Gans, Nathan Glazer, Joseph R. Gusfield, and Christopher Jencks (eds.). Philadelphia: University of Pennsylvania Press, 1979.

Glazer, Nathan and Daniel Patrick Moynihan. "Why Ethnicity?" *Commentary* 58, No. 4 (October, 1974).

Goffman, E. *Stigma: Notes on the Management of Spoiled Identity*. Englewood Cliffs, New Jersey: Prentice-Hall, 1963.

Goldstein, Sidney. "American Jewry, 1980: A Demographic Profile." *American Jewish Yearbook 1982*. New York and Philadelphia: American Jewish Committee and Jewish Publication Society of America, 1981.

Goldstein, Sidney and Calvin Goldscheider. *Jewish Americans: Three Generations in a Jewish Community*. Englewood Cliffs, New Jersey: Prentice-Hall, 1968.

Gordis, David M. Samuel Friedland Lectures. New York, 1974.

Greeley, Andrew M. *Ethnicity in the United States*. New York: American Jewish Committee, 1974.

Greenberg, Irving. "The Third Great Cycle in Jewish History." *Perspectives*. New York. (September, 1981).

——. "Will There Be One Jewish People by the Year 2000?" National Jewish Resource Center. New York, 1985.

Hall, Calvin S. and Gardner Lindzey. *Theories of Personality*. New York: Wiley, 1970.

Hansen, Marcus L. "The Third Generation in America," *Commentary* 14, No. 5 (November, 1952).

Herman, Simon N. "Criteria for Jewish Identity," *World Jewry in the State of Israel*. Arno Press, 1977.

——. *Jewish Identity*. Beverly Hills: Sage, 1977.

Heschel, Abraham J. "Existence and Celebration." Address to the 34th General Assembly, Council of Jewish Federations and Welfare Funds. Montreal. November 13, 1965.

Himmelfarb, Harold S. "The Impact of Religious Schooling: the Effect of Jewish Education Upon Adult Religious Involvement." unpublished Doctoral Dissertation. University of Chicago, 1974.

——. "Jewish Education for Naught: Educating the Culturally Deprived Jewish Child," *Analysis* No. 51 (September 1975).

Himmelfarb, Harold S. and R. Michael Loar. "National Trends in Jewish Ethnicity: A Test of the Polarization Hypothesis." *Journal for the Scientific Study of Religion* (1984).

Himmelfarb, Milton. "Like Everyone Else, Only More So?" *The Jews of Modernity*. New York: Basic Books, 1973.

Hochberg, Hillel. "Trends and Developments in Jewish Education." *American Jewish Yearbook 1973*. New York and Philadelphia: American Jewish Committee and Jewish Publication Society of America, 1972.

Hollingshead, August B., and Frederick C. Redlich. *Social Class and Mental Illness: A Community Study*. New York, Wiley 1958.

Huberman, Steven. "Synagogue Affiliating in the Los Angeles Jewish Community." Jewish Federation Council of Greater Los Angeles, 1984.

Jerusalem Institute of Federal Studies. "Are American Jews Becoming Conservatives and Should They?" *Viewpoints* (May, 1981).

"Jewish Los Angeles." Community Priorities System Report Number 1. Jewish Federation Council of Greater Los Angeles, 1982.

Jewish Post and Opinion. April 24, 1981.

Jewish Telegraph Agency. "Two-Decade Enrollment Decline in Jewish Schools is Leveling Off." November 7, 1979.

Johnson, George (ed.). "Zero Population Growth and the Jewish Community: A Symposium." *Analysis* No. 60 (November-December 1976).

Kaplan, Mordecai M. *Judaism as a Civilization: Towards a Reconstruction of American-Jewish Life*. New York: Macmillan, 1934.

Kelman, Herbert C. "The Place of Jewish Identity in the Development of Personal Identity." A report. Harvard University. Cambridge, Mass., October, 1980.

Klein, Judith Weinstein. *Jewish Identity and Self-Esteem*. New York: American Jewish Committee, September, 1980.

Lazerwitz, Bernard. *Contemporary Jewry* IV, No. 2 (Spring/Summer, 1967).

Lazerwitz, Bernard and Michael Harrison. "American Jewish Denominations: A Social and Religious Profile." *American Sociological Review* 44 (1979).

Lenski, Gerhard. *The Religious Factor*. Garden City, New York: Anchor Books, 1963.

Lewin, Kurt. *Resolving Social Conflict*. New York: Harper, 1948.

Lidz, Theodore. *The Person*. New York: Basic Books, 1968.

Lieber, David. "A Time for Taking Stock." paper delivered at seminar sponsored by the University of Judaism and the Western States Region of the Rabbinic Assembly. Idylwild, California. August 15, 1977.

Liebman, Charles S. "American Jewry: Identity and Affiliation." *The Future of the Jewish Community in America*. ed. by David Sidorsky. New York: Basic Books, 1973.

Lipstadt, Deborah E. *Judaism* 30, No. 3 (Summer, 1981).

Los Angeles Times. October 13, 1984.

Marden, Charles F. and Gladys Meyer. *Minorities in American Society*. New York: The Van Nostrand Reinhold Co., 1968.

Massarik, Fred. "A Report on the Jewish Population of Los Angeles 1968." Jewish Federation Council of Greater Los Angeles, 1968.

——. "Intermarriage: Facts for Planning." *National Jewish Population Study*. New York: Council of Jewish Federations and Welfare Funds, 1973.

Massarik, Fred and Alvin Chenkin. "United States National Jewish Population Study: The First Report." *American Jewish Yearbook 1974,* New York and Philadelphia: American Jewish Committee and Jewish Publication Society of America, 1973.

Mayer, Egon. *Love and Tradition,* New York: Plenum Publishing Co., 1985.

Metropolitan Atlanta Jewish Population Study. Atlanta Jewish Federation. Atlanta, Georgia, 1985.

Motz, Annabel Bender. "Commentaries on Selected Writings of Marshall Sklare." *Contemporary Jewry* 4, No. I (Fall/Winter, 1977-78).

Murphy, G. and R. Likert. *Public Opinion and the Individual*. New York: Harper and Bros., 1937.

Narell, Irena. "Northern California." *Present Tense* (Spring, 1982).

Newsweek. March 1, 1971.

Newsweek. October 4, 1982.

New York Times. "Poll Finds 40% Worship Regularly." December 30, 1979.

Novak, Michael. *Further Reflections on Ethnicity*. Middletown, Pennsylvania: Jednota Press, 1977.

Ostow, Mortimer. "The Pschological Determinants of Jewish Identity." *The Israel Annals of Psychology and Related Disciplines* 15, No. 4 (December, 1977).

Parenti, Michael. "Ethnic Politics and the Persistence of Ethnic Identification." *American Political Science Review*. (September, 1967).

Phillips, Bruce A. "Planning and Demographic Data from Community Telephone Survey." A Report to the Planning and Budgeting Department of the Jewish Federation Council of Greater Los Angeles. January 16, 1980.

——. Phoenix Jewish Population Study. An interview. Phoenix, Arizona. 1984.

Phillips, Bruce A. and Eleanor P. Judd. "The Denver Jewish Population Study,

1981." The Allied Jewish Federation of Denver, 1981.
Phillips, Bruce A. and Eve Weinberg. "The Milwaukee Jewish Population: Report of a Survey." Policy Research Corporation. Chicago, 1984.
Potok, Chaim. *Wanderings*. New York: Fawcett-Crest Books, 1978.
Present Tense. "Rabbinical Movers and Shakers." 9, No. 3 (Spring, 1982).
Ritterband, Paul and Steven M. Cohen. *The Jewish Population of Greater New York, A Profile*. Federation of Jewish Philanthropies of New York, 1984.
Rochlin, Harriet and Fred. *Pioneer Jews,* Boston: Houghton Mifflin, 1984.
Rosenfield, Geraldine. "The Polls: Attitudes Toward American Jews." *Public Opinion Quarterly* 46 (1982):
Sandberg, Neil C. *Ethnic Identity and Assimilation: The Polish-American Community*. New York: Praeger Publishers, 1974.
——, *Stairwell 7: Family Life in the Welfare State,* Beverly Hills: Sage, 1978.
Sass, Stephen J. "Southern California." *Present Tense* (Spring, 1982).
Schmelz, U. O. "Jewish Survival: The Demographic Factors." *American Jewish Yearbook 1981*. New York and Philadelphia: American Jewish Committee and Jewish Publication Society of America, 1980.
Schneider, William. "Anti-Semitism and Israel: A Report on American Public Opinion." unpublished paper. New York: American Jewish Committee, December, 1978.
Schulweis, Harold. "The Holocaust Dybbuk." *Moment* I, No. 7 (February, 1976).
Sebald, Hans. *Adolescence: A Sociological Analysis*. New York: Appleton-Century-Crofts, 1968.
Sidorsky, David. *The Future of the Jewish Community in America*. New York: Basic Books, 1973.
Silberman, Charles E. "Goals and Practice in Jewish Education: A Personal Perspective." American Jewish Committee Colloquium on Jewish Education and Jewish Identity. New York. June 9, 1975.
——. *A Certain People*. New York: Summit Books, 1985.
Sklare, Marshall and Joseph Greenblum. *Jewish Identity on the Suburban Frontier*. New York: Basic Books, 1967.
Sklare, Marshall, Marc Vosk and Mark Zborowski. "Forms and Expression of Jewish Identification." *Jewish Social Studies* XVII (1955).
Sleeper, James A. "A Radical View of Jewish Culture." *The Future of the Jewish Community in America*. ed. by David Sidorsky. New York: Basic Books, 1973.
Thurstone, L. L. "Attitudes Can Be Measured." *The American Journal of Sociology* 33, No. 4 (January, 1928).
Tobin, Gary A. "Demographic and Attitudinal Study of the St. Louis Jewish Population." unpublished mimeo. St. Louis, Missouri, 1982.
U.S. Census Bureau. Survey of 45,000 Households in 50 States and the District of Columbia. Washington, D.C., 1972.
Vorspan, Max and Lloyd T. Gartner. *History of the Jews of Los Angeles*. San Marino, California: The Huntington Library, 1970.
Warner, W. Lloyd. *American Life*. Chicago: University of Chicago Press, 1953.
Waxman, Chaim. "The Fourth Generation Grows Up: The Contemporary American Jewish Community." *Annals,* AAPSS, 454 (March, 1981).
Weisberg, Harold. "Ideologies of American Jews." *The American Jew*. ed. by Oscar I. Janowsky. Philadelphia: Jewish Publication Society of America, 1964.
Woocher, Jonathan S. "The 'Civil Judaism' of Communal Leaders." *American Jewish Yearbook 1981*. New York and Philadelphia: American Jewish Committee and Jewish Publication Society of America, 1980.

Yaffe, Richard. "Prophets Who Saw Jews Fading Decade Ago Probably Wrong." *B'nai B'rith Messenger*. July 11, 1980.

Yancy, William L. and Ira Goldstein. The Jewish Population of the Greater Philadelphia Area," Federation of Jewish Agencies of Greater Philadelphia. November 15, 1984.

Yankelovich, Daniel. "New Rules in American Life: Searching for Self-Fulfillment in a World Turned Upside Down." *Psychology Today* (April 1981).

Zimmer, Basil. "Participation of Migrants in Urban Structures." *American Sociological Review* (1955).

Index

About the Author

Neil C. Sandberg is a Fellow of the Center for Contemporary Jewish Life at the University of Judaism. He lectures on Jewish, cultural, and intergroup concerns at the Hebrew Union College and is professor of sociology at Loyola Marymount University in Los Angeles. As western regional director of the American Jewish Committee, he is an advisor on Jewish affairs and community relations to religious, civic, and government institutions. He is author of *Ethnic Identity and Assimilation: The Polish-American Community* (1974), *Stairwell 7: Family Life in the Welfare State* (1978), *Identity and Assimilation: The Welsh-English Dichotomy* (1981), and co-editor of *New Towns: Why—And For Whom?* (1973).